SpringerBriefs in Law

More information about this series at http://www.springer.com/series/10164

Cláudio Lucena

Collective Rights and Digital Content

The Legal Framework for Competition, Transparency and Multi-territorial Licensing of the New European Directive on Collective Rights Management

 Springer

Cláudio Lucena
Law Faculty
Paraíba State University
Paraiba
Brazil

ISSN 2192-855X   ISSN 2192-8568 (electronic)
SpringerBriefs in Law
ISBN 978-3-319-15909-6   ISBN 978-3-319-15910-2 (eBook)
DOI 10.1007/978-3-319-15910-2

Library of Congress Control Number: 2015932436

Springer Cham Heidelberg New York Dordrecht London
© The Author(s) 2015
This work is subject to copyright. All rights are reserved by the Publisher, whether the whole or part of the material is concerned, specifically the rights of translation, reprinting, reuse of illustrations, recitation, broadcasting, reproduction on microfilms or in any other physical way, and transmission or information storage and retrieval, electronic adaptation, computer software, or by similar or dissimilar methodology now known or hereafter developed.
The use of general descriptive names, registered names, trademarks, service marks, etc. in this publication does not imply, even in the absence of a specific statement, that such names are exempt from the relevant protective laws and regulations and therefore free for general use.
The publisher, the authors and the editors are safe to assume that the advice and information in this book are believed to be true and accurate at the date of publication. Neither the publisher nor the authors or the editors give a warranty, express or implied, with respect to the material contained herein or for any errors or omissions that may have been made.

Printed on acid-free paper

Springer International Publishing AG Switzerland is part of Springer Science+Business Media (www.springer.com)

To the People of Paraíba, my home State, who financed my studies and this research through our State University UEPB, an institution of which I could not be prouder to be part of, and which has been changing lives by offering free higher education for almost 50 years in a region of Brazil where education, hope and freedom happen to mean the very same thing.

Preface

The purpose of this study is to analyze to what extent collective rights management legal provisions reflect and accommodate the paradigmatic shifts in social behavior and in the ways of producing, consuming, and administrating intellectual content subject to copyright protection, changes that were brought by the technological development, digital tools and interaction mechanisms introduced in recent years. It assesses from a critical perspective the legal framework, particularly the recently introduced European Directive 2014/26/EU on collective management of copyright and related rights and multi-territorial licensing of rights in musical works for online use in the internal market, as well as other instruments that are available to discipline the issue, in order to determine strengths, weaknesses, and possible improving directions for the existing legal model of management of rights over the digital use of protected human creation.

The work starts contextualizing the environment of networked digital technologies in which the investigation takes place, where first information, and then interconnection is considered one of the main social assets, to understand the reasons, structures, mechanisms and channels that allow the paradigmatic shift in human behavior from two basic points of view. The first one is the broader shift in the way this new social architecture communicates, interacts, demands, produces and distributes information and impacts in economy, politics, citizenship and other general aspects. The second one is the more particular, legally-related impact of the wide sharing and collaboration possibilities that technologies introduce in the creation of artistic, scientific, and literary content, and consequently, in the ordinary economic, cultural, and legal notion of intellectual property.

In the following chapter, prior to initiating the legal analysis of the theme, the advent of digital technologies and how they allow new forms of social expression is covered. Collaborative mechanisms that are made possible through this enhanced social interaction are examined, and their economic dimension is identified as opportunities that emerge both in the form of the sharing logic of the discussed collaboration model, and in the disruptive effects that the creation and introduction of digital technologies may have in various aspects of everyday life.

The subsequent chapter turns eyes to digital networked and collaborative technologies in their particular projections in the creative industry, and how they irradiate effects so as to be perceived as relevant legal circumstances and addressed by legal mechanisms.

Chapter 4 analyzes the specificities of the activity of collective management of rights over digital content, primarily from the perspective of the relationship between Collective Management Organizations (CMOs) and the authors they represent. Since it is an essentially intermediation activity, it is inevitable to touch, and at times focus on their relationship with the publishers and the consumers who should be the final recipients and users of the service that these entities intermediate. Issues of transparency, accountability, and alternatives to multi-territorial licensing have been points of strong criticism and tension involving these undertakings, and especial attention will be devoted at the end of this section to analyze how these main controversial aspects were addressed in the scope of the new European Directive 2014/26/EU, which recently imposed significant transformations in this legal framework. The study is essentially an attempt to understand and analyze the differences between how the controversial issues of transparency and multi-territorial licensing were addressed before the entry into force of Directive 2014/26/EU and how they should be addressed after the adoption of the new legislation.

At the end it was possible to conclude that although digital networked and collaborative tools exponentially enlarged the possibilities of electronic use of creative content, the inability of CMOs to give better responses to modern market demands and, in consequence, to provide better services puts them in a delicate business position and defies their legitimacy to continue as intermediating agents between artists and content users. Insisting merely in traditional practices for the management of rights over new forms of electronic use of creative content will not allow these undertakings to attain the necessary level of efficiency and will create serious obstacles for them to preserve the viability of their economic activity. In spite of the impossibility to reach a conclusive position, since the Directive has just been adopted and transposition procedures by Member States have only started, it is possible to conclude that, by adopting a new framework addressing, among other important aspects, transparency concerns and multi-territorial licensing of online works, the new European Directive 2014/26/EU creates sufficient conditions and improves legal certainty so that CMOs can provide better and more efficient services from which every player in the field can benefit, while at the same time fulfills a historic demand from artists and users concerning the enhancement of the monitoring and control over the operation of these companies.

Contents

1	**Introduction**.	1
	References	3
2	**Shift Happens**	5
	2.1 Digital Technologies Allow New Forms of Social Interaction.	6
	2.2 Enhanced Interaction Opens New Collaboration Possibilities	7
	2.3 A New Collaboration Model Presents New Economic Opportunities.	8
	2.3.1 Sharing Economy and Disruptive Innovation.	10
	References	12
3	**Why Does Law Even Care?**	13
	3.1 The Scale of the Economic Repercussion of the Creation Industry	14
	3.2 Technology Itself Can Play a Regulatory Role.	16
	3.3 Legal Interests at Stake and the *Mantra* of Balance	17
	References	20
4	**Collective Rights Management**	21
	4.1 Collecting in the Name of the Artist.	22
	4.2 Controversial Issues in the Context of Collective Rights Management	24
	4.2.1 Competition Issues.	24
	4.2.2 Transparency and Accountability	25
	4.2.3 Multi-territorial Licensing	29

		4.3	The Legal Framework of the Collective Rights Management (CRM) Directive.............	30
			4.3.1 Competition Issues................	32
			4.3.2 Transparency and Accountability........	34
			4.3.3 Multi-territorial Licensing...........	37
	4.4		Creators X Creative Industry—Are We Speaking the Same Language?.................	41
	References............................			43
5	**Conclusion**............................			45
	References............................			47
Bibliography...............................				49

Abbreviations

CMO	Collective Management Organization
ECJ	European Court of Justice
EU	European Union
ICESCR	International Covenant on Economic, Social and Cultural Rights
ICT	Information and Communication Technology
IFTI	International Federation of the Phonographic Industry
MS	Member State
The Commission	The European Commission
UDRH	Universal Declaration on Human Rights
WIPO	World Intellectual Property Organization
WTO	World Trade Organization

Chapter 1
Introduction

When developments of *sociodigitization*[1] reasonably stabilize and finally accommodate in our daily lives on a fairly uniform way throughout a growingly globalized world, it will most probably seem the Industrial Revolution had no more than the effect of a small bumper in the history of men. It is the deepest and fastest global, man-driven transformation of all times, with obvious impacts in all fields of human existence, from economy to behavior, from culture to politics, from artistic expression to science.

Technologies have been an important component driving human behavior throughout history. In past decades, particularly, Information and Communication Technologies (ICTs) have played a very important role in this scenario. Two recent technological states can be pointed out to contextualize how this technical advances impact and shape different social configurations.

The first state can be identified as a moment when this set of tools, channels, and equipments is merely referred to as *Information Technologies*, which at their time were able to provide information flow in such a way as to start having significant impact in economic, political, and cultural activity. The social asset at this moment is the information itself.[2]

The second state is a moment when the new digital ecosystem starts to be referred to as being based on *Information and Communication Technologies*, since they begin redirecting the massive one-way flow of information to full interaction experiences, making extensive use of sharing and collaboration mechanisms, and transforming interconnection, not only information, by itself, into the new social commodity.[3] It is a paradigmatic shift in human behavior with clearly perceptible, concrete, and relevant effects, among others, in communication, economy, and law.

---

[1] Latham and Sassen (2005) use the term to refer to a process of transformation through which the logics of social organization, interaction, and space is affected by digitized information and communication structures and dynamics.
[2] Fritz Machlup has been one of the first to use the term *Information Society*. *Knowledge society* is also used. Machlup (1980).
[3] Castells (2006), Chapter I, p. 56.

© The Author(s) 2015
C. Lucena, *Collective Rights and Digital Content*,
SpringerBriefs in Law, DOI 10.1007/978-3-319-15910-2_1

Digital technologies fostering collaboration impacted deeper than ever in all aspects of human life, and for the purposes of this study, there is particular interest in the way they transformed the expression of creativity and, more specifically, the production of intellectual content. Back in the 18th century an economic activity started to be organized around the collective management of artists' rights, through intermediation with users, a business that has been prospering ever since due to never-ending human creativity and sensibility for artistic expression, basic sources of its input. It is an activity that, like any other, has its importance and its points of tension, debate, and disagreement. Like any other relevant human endeavor, it has developed its own ordinary legal structure, subject to compliance and enforcement procedures and has also developed its characteristic microsystem of contractual principles, conditions and transactions, responsibilities, infringements, jurisdiction, and litigation.

This microsystem was challenged, and proved not to be sufficient when digital technologies exponentially enlarged the possibilities of using and exploring rights derived from human creation in the digital environment, when existing structures failed to provide services in the scale and at the speed that the new market and actors demanded. While digital networks, collaboration technologies, and the sharing logic of a new world opened the doors to multiple opportunities of use (economic or not) for electronic content, the activity that managed those opportunities saw itself limited both in operation and management.

As for management, collecting societies have long been addressed criticism due to the lack of transparency in their business practices. As intermediating agents, they are supposed to provide the artists whose rights they manage adequate information on the managed rights, what was never a strong point in the history of these organizations. Operational difficulties also mounted. In Europe, for example, as the process of integration advanced, due to legal uncertainty of territorial restrictions and lack of adequate frameworks these organizations experienced growing difficulties to promote and explore cross-border uses of works that in substance have a natural tendency for global reach.

And when it all went digital, problems started to border the unbearable. Artists are now more and more *Digital Natives*.[4] They have grown up with these technologies as part of their lives as daily tools, as evident and natural resources and mechanisms which are necessary to play, develop, learn, travel, communicate, inform, interact, socialize, relate, date, and now work. It is difficult for them to see that an ordinary instrument used in the creative work they produce is not incorporated in the service of those who manage this work for them, causing dissatisfaction, inefficiency, and loss of revenue. Proper understanding and clear discipline of the main issues concerning the management of artists' rights in the digital environment is essential to address this anachronism.

---

[4] Prensky addresses the issue from the point of view that even brain cells organization configures differently depending on the received stimuli (Prensky 2001).

The Digital Agenda initiative has identified this proper addressing as an important step to achieve full integration in the Single market, a step which the European Commission and other stakeholders are trying to advance through an improved legal framework that attempts to redesign some traditional concepts in the field of intellectual property and particularly in the activity of collective management of artists' rights. The administration of such rights in the digital environment demands adaptation to the logics of the network society technologies so that those who explore an economic activity of this nature are able to offer more transparent, more dynamic, more individualized and, in general, smarter and better services.

References

Castells M (2006) La Sociedad Red
Latham R, Sassen S (2005) Digital formations: constructing an object of study. Digital formations. IT and new architectures in the Global Realm. Princeton University Press, Princeton. http://press.princeton.edu/chapters/i7992.html. Accessed 29 July 2005
Machlup F (1980) Knowledge: its creation, distribution, and economic significance, Volume I: Knowledge and knowledge production. Princeton University Press, Princeton
Prensky M (2001) Digital natives, digital immigrants. http://www.marcprensky.com/writing/Prensky-DigitalNatives,DigitalImmigrants–Part1.pdf

Chapter 2
Shift Happens

Transformation in nature is permanent. The course of mankind on the planet is no exception. If not for any other reason, only for man's natural inclination and tendency to adapt to the environment, but also to adapt the environment to his needs. Yet, both the pace and the amplitude of changes in the social environment in recent years is unprecedented in our history, technical development playing a leading role in the construction of this new reality with its capability of penetrating in substantially all domains of human activity as an external source of impact.[1]

It is in fact accurate to say that technical development has acted as protagonist in many, if not in all of the major recent moments in time when social structures were forced to turn route. It has been so, for instance, concerning the use of new sources of energy during successive periods and phases when the Industrial Revolution[2] led to a social, political, and economic turning point. But never in history have the transformations hit so hard, so fast and so wide as it has been the case with Information and Communication Technologies (ICTs) that have been developed, experienced, and incorporated into the daily lives of this generation, particularly those tools that have appeared and made their way in the two past decades.

These are certainly not the first significant technical developments that impacted in the dissemination of information and knowledge that history records. The advent of the press in China, and later in Europe, for example, had evident revolutionary consequences in this field. Modern technologies, however, feature an unparalleled characteristic of convergence that combined with the stage of technical development when these facts take place, provides the necessary conditions for the effects of these technologies to hit social structures more vertically, more horizontally and especially more rapidly than ever seen before.

Efforts to describe this new paradigm of social organizations have focused on the importance of information (Information Society) or knowledge (Knowledge Society) as their fundamental assets. The terminology resulting from this is unsatisfactory due to the fact that both information and knowledge have been central in all known societies. From another perspective, the way these technologies impacted on

---

[1] Castells (2006), Chapter I, p. 57.
[2] Ibid., pp. 1–3.

a well-known aspect of human of organization—the network—suggests a better description for the phenomenon. The observation that these developments have actually allowed networks to keep their historical strengths of flexibility and adaptability, while finally offering the tools to overcome coordination difficulties through sharing and collaboration possibilities led to the more meaningful depiction of the arrangement as *Network Society*.[3]

This social structure is the environment of the present study.

2.1 Digital Technologies Allow New Forms of Social Interaction

In the core of the various kinds of digital technologies and trends that paved the road of the network society—or rather drove alongside it—there has always been the idea of dematerialization.[4] Intangibility, the absence of physical or tactile constraints growingly became a prominent feature of a transformation process through which information and communication went in its earlier stages, and finally emerged as one characteristic that forced information and communication to be perceived differently from which they were in preceding analog-structured records.[5] This intangibility is of remarkable importance to the further developments specifically concerning the creative content that is the object of this study.

Besides that conceptual role, intangibility is also a condition that renders possible the emergence of another key characteristic, very unique to this new scene, which is the notion of something being able to exist anywhere at the same time, namely, ubiquity. Ubiquitous computing[6] is a still evolving concept according to which advances and innovation lead to a stage when we no longer perceive the interactions with technology for certain tasks, since we do not deliberately seek it in a particular moment or before a particular equipment like a desktop, as two or three generations frequently did. Instead, technology "recedes into the background of our lives"[7] and we engage in an almost unnoticed use of it through devices that are commonplace and incorporated to our everyday activities. Behind this idea is the reasoning that a computer, as an invisible servant, is in a better condition to help us perform regular activities and that since this external aid enables people to optimize their attention, it is supposed to create calmness. Ubiquitous computing and calm technology have made their way into the social structure, and their utility has even

---

[3] The Network Society From Knowledge to Policy Edited by Manuel Castells, Chapter I, Manuel Castells, p. 4.

[4] Lucchi (2006), p. 35.

[5] Ibid., p. 13.

[6] Weiser (2001).

[7] Weiser and Brown (1995) describe calm technology as "that which informs but doesn't demand our focus or attention".

secured them recognition of their importance in legal instruments,[8] but designers failed to foresee or did not properly refer to an adverse consequence which is also very common in ubiquity—torts and other infringements are also ubiquitous.[9] This is especially true for infringements that particularly interest this study in the further topics, because they are caused in the scope of the intellectual creation activity, itself frequently immaterial and ubiquitous.

Digital technologies also inaugurated a phase in which social expression also benefits from replication, transmission, storage and manipulation facilities, not to mention a priorly unthinkable nonlinearity and machine-equivalency in nature and form,[10] all at costs that could not even be imagined in previous stages of human development, an aspect that will also be object of analysis in following topics.

2.2 Enhanced Interaction Opens New Collaboration Possibilities

The nuances digital technologies brought into social interaction favored, as previously mentioned, the overcoming of a crucial difficulty that network structures have invariably faced to function adequately and efficiently, that was coordination. Two actions—sharing and collaborating—receive a whole new meaning in the reality of human interaction, whether we are referring to personal or professional interaction, exactly because digital technologies have put them into a whole new perspective.

Computers with enough power to process more and faster than ever, and that benefit from the new broad interconnection reality that begins to become available start laying the grounds to create "a platform for new kinds of collaborative human action and production."[11] Time and physical distances no longer impeded remote collaboration and from business and commerce to scientific research, from government initiatives to personal relationships, from industrial research to strategic decisions in all sectors, joint efforts and cooperation started to be sensed not only as a natural, but also as a useful and attractive interplay to promote common interests and/or achieve common results.

Shared knowledge and the potential to process, calculate, experience, cross-reference, evaluate, feedback and reevaluate has been consistently evolving and gaining weight in the domains of government and science development. "From philosophy to medicine, accounting to education, and town planning to social

---

[8] Directive 2014/26/EU, expressly recognizes, in (39) that, "in an era of online exploitation of musical works, commercial users need a licensing policy that corresponds to the ubiquity of the online environment and is multi-territorial".

[9] Lopez-Tarruella (2012), p. 345.

[10] Samuelson (1990), p. 324.

[11] Krikorian and Kapczynski (2010) mention Benkler (2006) and refer to experiences like Wikipedia and Free Software.

insurance, "know-how" and technology make modern governance possible."[12] Social Sciences themselves have undergone transformation as a result of the new interaction perspectives provided by these technologies, methodologies, and data processing possibilities. Quantitative Social Sciences are able to analyze "increasing quantities of diverse, highly informative data"[13] and researchers can growingly interoperate on a larger scale, managing interdisciplinary facilities, tasks, and research teams.

This collaboration and sharing model also means dynamics. Digital network technologies are able to induce and coordinate participation on a global scale, fostering what has proven to be a naturally vibrant, lively, and constantly changing environment. When collaboration reaches the very instrument itself that is used in the process, what has happened for example with *Wiki*, the authorship tool from which *Wikipedia* is built and that encompasses the "quintessential commons peer-based production project",[14] it reveals its virtually unlimited potential. Moreover, it is a social model that can also encourage values of democracy, since the possibility to use resources freely implies "improved participation in the production of information and information-dependent components of human development."[15]

Finally, it is a paradigm that relies, to an extensive degree, on values of free initiative. Collaboration in this environment is essentially voluntary and encouraged by the perception that no strong or mandatory commitment is demanded from the individual, what "increases the range and diversity of cooperative relations people can enter, and therefore of collaborative projects they can conceive of as open to them."[16] Successful initiatives concerning this aspect include the possibility of sharing the results of the collaboration process[17] and of adopting practices and contributing to decisions and positions that will benefit public interests to the detriment of private ones and reinforcing free initiative grounds upon which collaboration and sharing were proposed and grew to represent what they are today in the scope of human interaction.

2.3 A New Collaboration Model Presents New Economic Opportunities

It is evident that economic value arises from the understanding and then from the further organization and exploration of the innovative characteristics of such new arrangements. Collaborative mechanisms are capable of providing from the simple,

---

[12] Ibid.
[13] King (2014).
[14] Benkler (2006).
[15] Ibid., p. 14.
[16] Ibid., p. 9.
[17] Lopez-Tarruella (2012), p. 346.

2.3 A New Collaboration Model Presents New Economic Opportunities

more obvious and direct possibilities of allowing digital replication and transmission of information, to business models based on more sophisticated computational alternatives that can, to name a few, identify groups of like-minded people,[18] enable collective filtering, offer unmediated links and *post factum* gratuity payments, explore the insurance of experience goods and trust advertising, each and every one of them with solid economic potential that has only become operationally feasible and implementable once it was technically possible to access and process the significant amounts and diversity of digital data available today. These economic opportunities that rise as an outcome of collaborative initiatives conform a market with particular characteristics, among which "products that have a short life circle and are technically complex, the occurrence of standardization and a large need for product compatibility and interoperability"[19] may be highlighted.

In the particular scope of globalized financial markets, the advent of digital networked technologies resulted in a significant increase in the demand for credit, currency, equity, and commodity futures operations, among others, speeding transactions and amplifying the scale of connectivity, and that's not even the most prominent effect in the sector. The possibility of using combined computational processing capabilities and powerful financial applications especially designed to assist in the internal and external strategic decision-making process is probably the most striking use of digital tools in the sector. "This in turn has opened the way for an explosion in financial innovations, most famously in the area of derivatives."[20]

The fact that it is possible for these digital networked collaboration mechanisms to generate economic value also puts a competition dimension on the table. The access, manipulation, and extraction of economic value out of knowledge, as a true commodity, must meet the expectations of competition frameworks designed to protect consumers, other competitors, and the very structure of the market, with a view of maximizing social welfare and ensuring fair business practices. Thus, undertakings that engage in the economic activity that profits from this reality will have the repercussions of their commercial practices subjected to tests concerning the identification and analysis of market power, abuse, dominant position, barriers to newcomers, all of which evidently exceed the pure economic domain and can only be properly conducted with strong legal background,[21] an issue to which this study will return in a further topic.

In the international arena, stronger and developed economies have been constantly competing for the ability to access information and knowledge as unsubstitutable components in the processes of learning and innovating, knowing how dependable successful growth and development can be on a good performance in this effort. They "need access to the existing stocks of knowledge—such as the existing outputs of science and technological innovation—to speed up their ability

---

[18] Dolgin (2012).
[19] Lopez-Tarruella (2012), p. 13.
[20] Latham and Sassen (2005).
[21] Whish and Bailey (2014), p. 2.

to achieve something like parity in the global knowledge economy". For poorer regions, weaker or developing economies, that access is also important, but then as a more basic attempt to ensure the conditions for human development.[22]

As a final word in this reasoning, times of crisis, as has been the one through which Europe, for example, has been going in recent years, are fertile periods for business models that try to seize developing, unexplored economic opportunities to thrive. Currently it is particularly the case of those new ventures related to networked technologies and digital content. They can be especially important and helpful in the recovery from the recession period, since the chain of services and products that their activity trigger is much broader than strictly defined content industries.[23]

2.3.1 Sharing Economy and Disruptive Innovation

It would not be possible to imagine that such profound shifts in the way of establishing and conducting businesses on the basis of unprecedented collaboration and using digital technologies to manage network structures with efficiency and in a scale that was never imagined before would leave all sectors of the economy untouched and unaffected. New ideas with sharing at its core inevitably clash with long established business models, and no other result but harsh conflict could be expected.

To use a rather recent example, the functionalities of *UberPop*, a service offered by an American company that allows private drivers to offer themselves as chauffeurs through their *Uber's* taxi app connecting and sharing technology, triggered a legal battle in Brussels last April, in which a Taxi Drivers' Unions sought—and, to this date, managed—a court order to suspend the service, under grounds of unfair competition practice. The incident also gave rise to a severe and open conflict between public authorities, since while national officials seemed to be engaged in protecting the jobs and the activities of local formally registered taxi drivers, European Commission Vice-President and Commissioner for Digital Agenda Neelie Kroes vigorously criticized the decision, that ultimately represented, in her opinion, the protection of a cartel and an unjustifiable obstacle to innovation.[24] Legal questions aside for the time being, similar services like *BlaBlaCar* and *AirBnb*, that are already managing to monetize the sharing,[25] and many others that are still trying to keep operational in order to see what financial results can come

---

[22] Krikorian and Kapczynski (2010), p. 219.

[23] OECD (2010), p. 188.

[24] http://www.lefigaro.fr/secteur/high-tech/2014/04/16/01007-20140416ARTFIG00100-guerre-des-taxis-uber-partiellement-interdit-dans-les-rues-de-bruxelles.php. Accessed in August 5th, 2014.

[25] The Economist, Airbnb versus hotels Room for all, for now—But there are signs that the sharing site is starting to threaten budget hotels. Apr 26th 2014 | New York | From the print edition http://www.economist.com/news/business/21601259-there-are-signs-sharing-site-starting-threaten-budget-hotels-room-all Accessed in August 5th 2014.

2.3 A New Collaboration Model Presents New Economic Opportunities

next, do confront traditional entrenched economic activities, and may as well pose risk to their continuity. And not only does this happen to services, but also to products or simply methods. It is the normally painful manner through which things that have always been done a certain way start to be tried differently.

The perplexity is not new. Creative destruction,[26] disruptive innovation or the *Innovator's Dilemma* are all terminologies that have differently approached the question to describe the essential cornerstone circumstance at the base of every major step of technological progress: the fact that the very same technical improvements that open new opportunities, that drive the broadening of the horizons in the economic structures, and that does this repeatedly over time tend to do it at the expense of existing market players. Affected enterprises are normally huge organizations, leading undertakings of the sector in question, which will obviously attempt to resist change and remain in their comfort zone, trying to keep the *status quo* with the weapons at hand, a resistance which can make them lose ground and revenue in the long run, and which will not probably allow them to survive and escape market elimination in case the change is successful, unless considerable and extensive adjustments are made.

Digital technologies are the most recent disruptive innovation forces acting in the modern economy. Although its effects are not even close to have been thoroughly perceived, some particular sectors of the economy, as media, and even more specific activities or businesses, like traditional newspapers, have already felt their disruption power. Overall, it did not take long for the industry that produces and explores intellectual content, the activity which is ultimately the object of examination of this study, to recognize a corresponding *Digital Dilemma*[27]: "information in digital form is largely liberated from the medium that carries it". It is a challenge with which the content sector has to deal immediately if it wishes to outlive the digital revolution, because it completely subverts the whole logic, the very premise of dependency between content and physical support, upon which this economic activity was organized over the last centuries.

Only this time, due to the aforementioned intensity, depth, and width of the transformations, it seems that business models are not the only human intellectual activities to be affected. The dimension of the disruption is now such as to extend the current process of creative destruction even to the legal order, providing clear evidence that traditional legal regimes may no longer be appropriate or adequately responsive to the needs and challenges of the digital reality.[28]

---

[26] Schlesinger and Doyle (2014).
[27] Committee on Intellectual Property Rights and the Emerging Information Infra-structure, National Research Council (2000).
[28] Lucchi (2006), p. 140.

References

Benkler Y (2006) The wealth of networks. Yale University Press, Yale. http://www.benkler.org/Benkler_Wealth_Of_Networks.pdf

Castells M (2006) La Sociedad Red

Castells M, Cardoso G (2005) The network society from knowledge to policy, center for transatlantic relations

Committee on Intellectual Property Rights and the Emerging Information Infra-structure, National Research Council (2000) The digital dilemma: intellectual property in the information age. National Academy Press, Washington DC

Directive 2014/26/EU on collective management of copyright and related rights and multi-territorial licensing of rights in musical works for online use in the internal market

Dolgin A (2012) Manifesto of the new economy. Institutions and business models of the digital society. Springer, New York

King G (2014) Restructuring the social sciences: reflections from Harvard's Institute for Quantitative Social Science. Harvard University, Cambridge

Krikorian G, Kapczynski A (2010) Access to knowledge in the age of intellectual property. Zone Books, New York

Latham R, Sassen S (2005) Digital formations: constructing an object of study. Digital formations. IT and new architectures in the Global Realm. Princeton University Press, Princeton. http://press.princeton.edu/chapters/i7992.html. Accessed 29 July 2005

Lopez-Tarruella A (2012) Google and the law, empirical approaches to legal aspects of knowledge-economy business models. Springer, The Hague

Lucchi N (2006) Digital media and intellectual property—management of rights and consumer protection in a comparative analysis. Springer, Berlin

OECD (2010) The internet economy in the post-crisis era and recovery, in OECD, OECD information technology outlook 2010. OECD Publishing. doi:10.1787/it_outlook-2010-6-en

Samuelson P (1990) Digital media and the changing face of intellectual property law. Rutgers Comput Techol Law J 16:323. http://scholarship.law.berkeley.edu/facpubs/246

Schlesinger P, Doyle G (2014) CREATe working paper 2014/06. From organisational crisis to multiplatform salvation? Creative destruction and the recomposition of news media. Prepublished in online first 12 May 2014. doi:10.1177/1464884914530223. http://jou.sagepub.com/content/early/2014/05/07/1464884914530223

The Economist, Airbnb versus hotels room for all, for now—but there are signs that the sharing site is starting to threaten budget hotels, 26 April 2014, New York. From the print edition. http://www.economist.com/news/business/21601259-there-are-signs-sharing-site-starting-threaten-budget-hotels-room-all

Weiser (2001) The computer for the 21st century. https://www.ics.uci.edu/~corps/phaseii/Weiser-Computer21stCentury-SciAm.pdf

Weiser M, Brown JS (1995) Designing calm technology. http://www.ubiq.com/hypertext/weiser/calmtech/calmtech.htm

Whish R, Bailey D (2014) Competition law, 7th edn. Oxford University Press, Oxford

Chapter 3
Why Does Law Even Care?

In the previous chapter, prior to initiating the so to speak legal analysis of the theme, the advent of digital technologies and how they allow new forms of social interplay was covered. Collaborative mechanisms that are made possible through this enhanced social interaction were also examined, and it was possible to point out an economic dimension, in the form of opportunities that emerge both in the form of the sharing drive of the discussed collaboration model, and in the disruption that the creation and introduction of digital technologies may and have been causing in our lives.

The path that was chosen to approach the legal aspects of the issue may suggest this economic contour is the only one that is relevant to establish repercussions that are to be felt by Law. This impression is false, though. For as much as an economic extent is important to draw legal effects, and tempting as such a pragmatic approach may seem, it is by all means unacceptable to despise that the development and the incorporation of digital technologies in everyday human life both have paramount impact over the exercise of fundamental and personality rights, as well as over other non-economic values duly protected by Law, as the right to take part in cultural life and to enjoy the benefits of scientific progress and its applications.[1]

That being said, it is appropriate to conclude that the legal interest in digital technologies originates out of the simple and obvious insight that their effects and the behavioral transformations they induce in the social tissue can—and already do—interfere with the sphere of rights and obligations of both legal and natural persons.

That alone is enough for Law and its structures to care.

---

[1] Article 15 ICESCR, UN.

3.1 The Scale of the Economic Repercussion of the Creation Industry

In medio stat virtus. If it is improper to neglect other dimensions of the legal interest concerning digital technologies, it is equally inadequate to disregard the significancy of the economic component, mainly when these digital technologies are employed in the universe that is the object of this study, namely, the creation and distribution of artistic and scientific content. In the past centuries, powerful conglomerates and a strong industry sector were organized and have prospered around the economic dimension of creativity. That was only viable following the fact that it was possible to add economic value to an activity which essentially used human expression as its primary input. The first legal mechanisms concerning the matter in the 18th[2] century promptly established a clear economic dimension concerning the activity and did not hesitate to highlight that the entrepreneurial operation surrounding the artistic expression was to be unquestionably protected and supported by Law. It is difficult to imagine Intellectual Property and Copyright under the spotlight in the critical discussions they dominate today, had that option been different, for any reason.

This is not to say that all possible uses and transactions involving content, and more specifically digital content, are strictly commercial. Not only noncommercial uses are possible and welcome, they have been experienced, and as the economic debate evolves, even an economy of gratuity is considered, involving "economic exchanges which are unconventional in that goods and services are delivered without money but in the expectation that they will be paid for after being used."[3] Such schemes present alternatives to measure and consider other values, like symbolic exchange, happiness, time and emotional dynamics,[4] that in regular transactions are unusual to traditional economy, but that due to new arrangements and conditions—digital mechanisms and applied collaborative technologies amongst them—may have developed some sort of economic appreciability that can render them *monetizable*, even if potentially. This is to say that non-commercial does not always and necessarily mean non-economic.

But the plain, appreciable economic effect of digital technologies in markets gives a significant overview of its size and scale. Figures may not always enjoy a high degree of accuracy, and the very delimitation of what comprises digital economy is not itself a simple exercise, but recent attempts of estimation of the phenomenon reveal that "by 2016 the Internet economy in the G-20 economies will

---

[2] Dolgin arguments that the main concern of the Statute of Anne, 1710 was not the protection of the creation of authors in itself, but rather the protection of the rights of entrepreneurs, as a rigorously commercial instrument. He stresses that the text did not at all refer to authors or to questions concerning the protection of their creative expression, as such (Dolgin 2012, p. 44).

[3] Manifesto. The Gratuity Economy: Retrospective Payment and Group Motivation, p. 29.

[4] Ibid.

be worth USD 4.2 trillion (up from USD 2.3 trillion in 2010)," with Internet representing almost one tenth of the Gross Domestic Product (GDP) in South Korea and the United Kingdom, and its related economic activities growing at a rate that far exceeds the growth rates of conventional sectors.[5] In the European Union, digital technology related-industry corresponds to 4.8 % of the economy, what stands for 25 % of total Research and Development businesses, not to mention that the sector is not only important as such, but it is also a very important element behind the increase in general productivity rates.[6]

In business to consumer (B2C) e-commerce only, Asia is the largest region in the world, which can be largely credited to the size of the Chinese market, having achieved a turnover of 406.1 billion and a growth rate of 16.7 %, whereas Europe achieved a turnover of 363.1 billion, having grown 16.3 % and North America a turnover of 333.5 billion, recording a 6.0 % growth.[7]

Traditional activities obviously face enormous challenges to migrate into the digital economy. Newspapers, for instance, have been experiencing a considerable decline both in print circulation and in advertisement revenues in the past years all over the world. Yet, recent studies carried out in the United Kingdom through Big Data tools reveal that their average revenues are still over £20 billion.[8] To tackle the pitfall and resist in the field, players like Telegraph Media Group (TMG) have decided to face the operation of the print newspaper not anymore only in itself, but as "an essential part of a multi-platform business."[9] Taking steps in this direction, the company jumped from 14 % of income coming out of digital sales in 2006 to 47 % by 2011, in a period when the number of digital customers grew from 90,000 in 2006 to 267,000 in 2011, when the company's turnover achieved £427 million.[10]

A more specific look at the industry whose commodity is creative content reveals its noticeable importance. In 2007, global figures for digital games and music industry already indicated a yearly revenue of over USD 20 billion, while digital advertising amounted to approximately USD 50 billion, representing 10 % of total worldwide advertising.[11] In the European Union, where 1.4 million small

---

[5] Brussels, 4 March 2014 TAXUD D1/JT Digit/008/2014 Expert Group on Taxation of the Digital Economy Working Paper: Digital Economy—Facts and Figures Meeting to be held on 13–14 March 2014. https://www.bcgperspectives.com/content/articles/media_entertainment_strategic_planning_4_2_trillion_opportunity_internet_economy_g20/.

[6] http://ec.europa.eu/taxation_customs/resources/documents/taxation/gen_info/good_governance_matters/digital/2014-03-13_fact_figures.pdf.

[7] European E-commerce Grew by 16 % to €363 Billion in 2013. 6.7.2014. http://www.ecommerce-europe.eu/press/european-e-commerce-grew-by-16-to-363-billion-in-2013.

[8] Max Nathan and Anna Rosso with Tom Gatten, Prash Majmudar and Alex Mitchell, Measuring the UK's Digital Economy with Big Data. National Institute for Economic and Social Research, http://niesr.ac.uk/sites/default/files/publications/SI024_GI_NIESR_Google_Report12.pdf.

[9] CREAT-e Schlesinger and Doyle (2014).

[10] Ibid.

[11] OECD (2010).

and medium sized enterprises (SMEs) are Intellectual Property-related industries,[12] the sector stands up for 39 % of the global economic activity in the area, which represents an annual figure of €4.7 trillion, and for 26 % of all employment, corresponding to 56.5 million jobs.[13]

Diving even deeper and confining our investigation to the music industry only, almost 10 million people are directly and indirectly employed in the EU, and the economic output of the sector exceeds €500 million, or 4,2 % of the total share of GDP.[14] Interesting to notice that contrary to what lobby associations of record labels claim, worldwide music industry overall revenue has not declined, reaching almost USD 60 billion in 2011. In 2012, around 34 % of global revenue from the sector came from streaming, downloads and the exploitation of other digital channels.[15]

3.2 Technology Itself Can Play a Regulatory Role

Another important, yet much less explored aspect to consider when pondering the reasons for Law to engage in close interactions with digital technologies is that the degree of transformations they inaugurated is such as to create conditions to turn their own infrastructure—code, architecture, networks, improvements, restrictions, technical rules and other structural components—into elements that will integrate the legal framework, and thus directly serve the purpose of limiting or promoting values, prohibiting conducts, investigating behaviors, as a true and maybe the most effective control tool ever.

To this extent, technologies themselves constitute new grounds for social infrastructures, and *constitution* in the sense of "an architecture—not just a legal text but a way of life—that structures and constrains social and legal power, to the end of protecting fundamental values."[16] The forces driving this architecture, currently influenced by strong political and economic ingredients, will certainly use their power to push the structure in the directions of values that interest them. Governments and economic actors, for instance, need a digital space where their tasks are made more simple and efficient. By making it clearly possible to identify

---

[12] A Single Market for Intellectual Property Rights Boosting creativity and innovation to provide economic growth, high quality jobs and first class products and services in Europe. http://ec.europa.eu/internal_market/copyright/docs/ipr_strategy/COM_2011_287_en.pdf.

[13] Intellectual property rights intensive industries: contribution to economic performance and employment in the European Union Industry-Level Analysis Report, September 2013. A joint project between the European Patent Office and the Office for Harmonization in the Internal Market. http://ec.europa.eu/internal_market/intellectual-property/docs/joint-report-epo-ohim-final-version_en.pdf.

[14] Ibid., p. 7.

[15] Cammaerts et al. (2013), pp. 7–8.

[16] Lessig (2006), p. 4.

who is who, *doing what*, *when* and *where* in a digital space, a safer environment is built, in which both businesses' and State's interests and objectives, in general, are more easily attained.[17] By promoting or inducing the use and the adoption of certain technologies, it is currently possible to interfere directly, more precisely, with the regulation framework of life in legal systems.[18] It follows that the architecture of digital networked and collaborative technologies, or the "Code is a regulator in cyberspace because it defines the terms upon which cyberspace is offered. And those who set those terms increasingly recognize the code as a means to achieving the behaviors that benefit them best."[19]

The reasoning entirely applies to intellectual property. Digital technologies per se are not in principle subject to legal restrictions, although their inherent attributes allow them to exercise influence over a legal transaction in a much stricter way than an adjustment expressed by a contract would. That being said, they can play a more static, less active role in the protection of creative content should they, for instance, only prevent copying or access to other sorts of enduring uses of this content, or they can serve more dynamic purposes of encouraging and being a catalyst of deeper influence in developing "business models where rights-holders determine at their own discretion terms and conditions for access and use of their works and embed these rules in technical devices."[20]

3.3 Legal Interests at Stake and the *Mantra* of Balance

It has been previously said in the course of this work that digital networked and collaborative technologies have—and already do exercise—potential to project their effects in one's spheres of rights and obligations. Moreover, it has also been particularly demonstrated that these technologies are deeply linked with a variety of recently-born economic rights and regulatory aspects, in addition to fundamental and personality rights and other non-economic legally protected values, as the right to take part in cultural life and to enjoy the benefits of scientific progress and its applications. These interests are not the only possible ones in the digital environment, neither yet are limits between all of them well-defined. Complex and demanding comprehension, they frequently overlap and hardly ever accommodate properly without external intervention, which naturally has to come from Law, invested in this very important function of managing the conflicts that may arise from the coexistence of such high-profile interests.

Ordinary use of digital technologies can confront, among other interests, free initiative, economic rights and freedom of speech, moral rights and freedom of

---

[17] Ibid., p. 61.
[18] Ibid., p. 62.
[19] Ibid., p. 84.
[20] Lucchi (2006), p. 13.

expression, privacy and national security. A number of legal instruments and court decisions have been adopted in the European Union in attempts to manage the effects of the introduction of digital technologies in criminal,[21] commerce,[22] consumer,[23] data protection[24] and other matters, as well as their implications in jurisdictional issues[25] in various aspects of human life.

Relevant protected interests in Competition Law also present challenge as long as their adequate recognition and handling are concerned. Conclusions regarding, for instance, the dominant position of an undertaking, may be wrongfully biased and may not realize existing competitive restrictions when investigating companies whose activities are inserted in an absolutely new market environment, because purely conventional methods of analysis are employed in the observation. The traditional comprehension of concepts such as market share and abuse, the orthodox approach and the customary techniques may not be enough to reach adequate diagnostics in such new circumstances,[26] because it has not yet become clear if this new reality can be addressed, with minor adjustments, using the existing framework, or if present rules simply "obstruct the development of businesses in the knowledge economy" and are only suitable for an industrial economic model.[27]

Like in all other scopes above described, activities that involve production and distribution of creative content have already experienced as well a number of attempts to have rules laid down trying to discipline the effects of digital networking collaborative technologies.[28]

In the creative content scenario, most of the times the clashing is between economic and property rights from one side, and fundamental rights from the other

---

[21] Directive 2013/40/EU of the European Parliament and of the Council of 12 August 2013 on attacks against information systems and replacing Council Framework Decision 2005/222/JHA and Council of Europe—ETS No. 185—Convention on Cybercrime.

[22] Directive 2000/31/EC of the European Parliament and of the Council of 8 June 2000 on certain legal aspects of information society services, in particular electronic commerce, in the Internal Market ('Directive on electronic commerce').

[23] Directive 2011/83/EU of the European Parliament and of the Council of 25 October 2011 on consumer rights, amending Council Directive 93/13/EEC and Directive 1999/44/EC of the European Parliament and of the Council and repealing Council Directive 85/577/EEC and Directive 97/7/EC of the European Parliament and of the Council.

[24] Directive 95/46/EC of the European Parliament and of the Council of 24 October 1995 on the protection of individuals with regard to the processing of personal data and on the free movement of such data, which was already in the process of reform and which had its content controlled by decision C-131/12 of the European Court of Justice, Google Spain SL, Google Inc. v Agencia Española de Protección de Datos, Mario Costeja González.

[25] ECJ Joined cases C-585/08 and C-144/09—Pammer v Reederei Karl Schlüter GmbH & KG; Hotel Alpenhof GesmbH v Oliver Heller and Case C-523/10, Wintersteiger AG v Products 4U Sondermaschinenbau GmbH,.

[26] Lopez-Tarruella (2012), p. 14.

[27] Ibid., p. 8.

[28] Information Society Copyright Directive, Directive 2001/29/EC on the harmonisation of certain aspects of copyright and related rights in the information society, Article 5.

3.3 Legal Interests at Stake and the *Mantra* of Balance

side, not to mention the more elaborate discussions that concern the very nature of intellectual property and their connection/collision with fundamental rights,[29] whose intricacy could not be properly explored without exceeding the limits and scope of the present study. Far from being a solely academic debate, it is a very interesting and recently recurring conflict about which both national courts and the European Court of Justice have had the opportunity to express themselves more than once,[30] in rulings that concisely denote that the European framework of fundamental rights offers the tools for judges to "correct certain excesses when the basic values of copyright are lost sight of", as well as to guide copyright through the legitimacy crisis that it faces before public opinion.[31]

Almost a hundred sources were consulted for the elaboration of this study. Out of those whose authors decided to address the issue of how much protection there should be in the legal instruments regulating the matter, 100 % openly express their undoubted understanding that the provisions should be enforced in a *balanced* way such as to protect creators' moral and economic rights and stimulate the continuity of intellectual production, whereas preserving at the same time adequate conditions of public access to information, knowledge, cultural inclusion and participation. When announcing their interests, intentions and hopes, public institutions, industry representatives, consumer voices, policy makers and even judicial entities also follow the very same path. This unvarying, and one could even say radical commitment could lead to the conclusion that there are no gray areas, and thus no worries arising from dissent concerning this field. It is an impression that couldn't be more wrong and far from reality. In spite of the apparent consensus and the *mantra* of balance, conflicts abound, and more often than not regarding the same practical item of the debate: the exact point where *balance* should be set.

A great deal of this conflict may be due to the fact that balance is being inappropriately faced as an objective, a goal, an aim in itself in the scenario of intellectual property protection, rather than what it actually seems to represent much better: a test. Balance will never achieve the static condition of having found the materialization of perfect coexistence for the rights and obligations it seeks to modulate in this domain. It is horizon, not a destination. As long as the Rule of Law with its values remain, balance will be a never ending test to be applied every time a major technical improvement brings change to the intellectual property scene. A test that should be used to gauge and adjust expectations and commitments from all sides.

---

[29] According to Mylly, the most simplistic approach to this issue would be to consider intellectual property as a fundamental right as such, an elementary reasoning exercise of Article 27(2) of the UDHR, according to which "Everyone has the right to the protection of the moral and material interests resulting from any scientific, literary or artistic production of which he is the author". Similar conclusions could be extracted from Article 15(1)(c) of the ICESCR and from Article 17(2) of The EU Charter. This simplification is by far inadequate, since mentioned mechanisms place a positive protection obligation in the States, but with wide margin of appreciation to the scope of implementation (Mylly 2007, p. 197).

[30] ECJ. Case C-200/96.

[31] Geiger (2009), Chapter 2, p. 48.

References

Brussels, 4 March 2014 TAXUD D1/JT Digit/008/2014 expert group on taxation of the digital economy working paper: digital economy—facts and figures meeting to be held on 13–14 March 2014. http://ec.europa.eu/taxation_customs/resources/documents/taxation/gen_info/good_governance_matters/digital/2014-03-13_fact_figures.pdf

Cammaerts B, Mansell R, Meng B (2013) Media policy brief 9 copyright and creation. A case for promoting inclusive online sharing. The London School of Economics and Political Science, Department of Media and Communications, September 2013

Case C-200/96, Metronome Music v Music Point Hokamp (1998) ECR I-1953

Communication from the commission to the European Parliament, the council, the European economic and social committee and the committee of the regions. a single market for intellectual property rights—boosting creativity and innovation to provide economic growth, high quality jobs—and first class products and services in Europe. Brussels, 24 May 2011, COM (2011) 287 final, p 3. http://ec.europa.eu/internal_market/copyright/docs/ipr_strategy/COM_2011_287_en.pdf

Directive 2001/29/EC of the European Parliament and of the Council of 22 May 2001 on the harmonisation of certain aspects of copyright and related rights in the information society

Dolgin A (2012) Manifesto of the new economy. Institutions and business models of the digital society. Springer, New York

European E-commerce grew by 16% to €363 billion in 2013. 6.7.2014. http://www.ecommerce-europe.eu/press/european-e-commerce-grew-by-16-to-363-billion-in-2013

Geiger C (2009) In: Derclaye E (ed) Research handbook on the future of EU copyright. Edward Elgar, Cheltenham. SSRN:http://ssrn.com/abstract=1316113

Intellectual property rights intensive industries: contribution to economic performance and employment in the European Union Industry-Level Analysis Report, September 2013. A joint project between the European Patent Office and the Office for Harmonization in the Internal Market. http://ec.europa.eu/internal_market/intellectual-property/docs/joint-report-epo-ohim-final-version_en.pdf

Lessig L (2006) Code version 2.0. Basic Books

Lopez-Tarruella A (2012) Google and the law. Empirical approaches to legal aspects of knowledge-economy business models. Springer, The Hague

Lucchi N (2006) Digital media and intellectual property—management of rights and consumer protection in a comparative analysis. Springer, Berlin

Mylly T (2007) Intellectual property and fundamental rights: do they interoperate? p 197

OECD (2010) The internet economy in the post-crisis era and recovery, in OECD, OECD information technology outlook 2010. OECD Publishing. doi:10.1787/it_outlook-2010-6-en

Nathan M, Rosso A, Gatten T, Majmudar P, Mitchell A Measuring the Uk's digital economy with big data. National Institute for Economic and Social Research. http://niesr.ac.uk/sites/default/files/publications/SI024_GI_NIESR_Google_Report12.pdf

Schlesinger P, Doyle G (2014) CREATe working paper 2014/06. From organisational crisis to multiplatform salvation? Creative destruction and the recomposition of news media. Prepublished in online first 12 May 2014. doi:10.1177/1464884914530223 http://jou.sagepub.com/content/early/2014/05/07/1464884914530223

Chapter 4
Collective Rights Management

Previous chapters described networked digital and collaborative technologies, their social and economic impact, their particular projections in the creative industry, and how they irradiate effects so as to be both perceived as relevant legal circumstances and addressed by legal mechanisms. The next topics will be dedicated to understand and analyze the specificities of the activity of collective rights management, primarily from the perspective of the relationship between Collective Management Organizations (CMOs) and the authors they represent. Since it is an essentially intermediation activity, it is inevitable to touch, and at times to focus on their relationship with the publishers and the consumers who should be the final recipients and users of the service that these entities intermediate. Issues of transparency, accountability, and alternatives to multi-territorial licensing have been points of strong criticism and tension involving these undertakings, and especial attention will be devoted at the end of this section to analyze how the main controversial aspects of the new European Directive 2014/26/EU, which recently imposed significant transformations in this legal framework,[1] addressed these most disputed matters.

The new Directive and the new framework for collective rights management is a concrete outcome of the course set by the European Commission in 2010, when it launched the Digital Agenda for Europe,[2] a policy through which the institution expressly recognized the strategical potential of Information and Communication Technologies (ICTs) and their importance in fully implementing a Single Market. In view of the difficulties brought by the economic crisis, envisaging the overcoming of structural weaknesses and resuming the path of progress, the announced objective of the Agenda was "to deliver sustainable economic and social benefits from a digital single market based on fast and ultra fast internet and interoperable applications."[3] To achieve the proclaimed goal, a series of actions should be taken,

---

[1] Directive 2014/26/EU on collective management of copyright and related rights and multi-territorial licensing of rights in musical works for online use in the internal market.
[2] Communication from the Commission to the European Parliament, the Council, the European Economic and Social Committee and the Committee of the Regions. A Digital Agenda for Europe /* COM/2010/0245 f/2 */.
[3] Ibid., 1. Introduction.

© The Author(s) 2015
C. Lucena, *Collective Rights and Digital Content*,
SpringerBriefs in Law, DOI 10.1007/978-3-319-15910-2_4

among which the opening of access to content in the EU with the introduction of legislation that promoted simplification and enhancement of the efficiency of collective rights management, as well as facilitated multi-territorial licensing so as to permit online music services to be offered without having to negotiate with numerous rights management societies based in 27 countries.[4] In the past years, European Commission Vice President and Commissioner for Digital Agenda, Neelie Kroes has demonstrated intense personal engagement in the initiatives related to the implementation of the Digital Agenda, having recently expressed that "The single market is the EU's crown jewel, and online is its natural new home."[5]

4.1 Collecting in the Name of the Artist

Before delving into more intricate legal reflections, it seems opportune to stress the rather forward thinking behind the idea of structuring an organized activity that consists in the collection and administration of revenue in the name of artists who personally hold economic rights over their creation. For a number of reasons, there undoubtedly was a refined sense of opportunity in the first place back in the days[6] of the conception of the idea of establishing an intermediation business to connect authors and users who were interested in the content they created. For as much as both commercial and interpersonal relationships were at the time much different from today, it certainly took an ingenious insight to perceive the conditions that favored the launching of a business model that would thrive for decades to come, in spite of the difficulties it would have to face along the years.

It is also an interesting exercise to examine these conditions in light of the reform through which the system is going, because paradigmatic transformations are currently happening in the business and its legal model exactly because the catalyst of the changes, that is to say, digital networked technologies, have affected those original circumstances more intensely than ever before, imposing evolution and adaption to a new reality.

The basic favorable condition for the collecting activity to prosper was that the business transactions involving the use of the creative content were not the end activity of the artist. The prospection of clients or users, negotiation of contracts,

---

[4] Ibid., 2.1.1.

[5] Kroes (2014).

[6] First records of collective management of theatrical, dramatic and literary works of artists rights date back to 1777, in France. The activity expanded specifically to the music market in 1850, when a similar organization was established, also in France. Collective management societies are now present in over 100 countries. Collective Management in Reprography, World Intellectual Property Organization (WIPO) and the International, 2004 Federation of Reproduction Rights Organisations (IFRRO). http://www.ifrro.org/upload/documents/wipo_ifrro_collective_management.pdf.

and administration of revenue, not to mention all the bureaucratic burden these tasks carry along, have always being time-consuming efforts that more often than not also require particular abilities and competences which artists do not usually possess and rarely appreciate exercising. The premise that outsourcing these duties would allow the artists to devote extended time and attention to fully concentrate on the expression of their talent certainly seemed valid and attractive.

An underlying condition for the success of the newborn activity that envisaged the exploitation of immaterial assets which had just been recognized economic value not long before was the fact that individual contact between artists and each and every potential user for the purposes of reproduction, public performance, and communication of their work was then also operationally difficult, if not absolutely impracticable. It must be added that as time went by, once it had become usual for creative content to be fixed to some sort of physical support, the tasks of individually monitoring the use and enforcing authors' rights also growingly became virtually impossible, what ended up reinforcing the convenience of a collective representation system, imperfect as it might be.

As a matter of fact these imperfections have always been there, and have always faced criticism, to some extent. Actually, the business model already carried in its very conception the seeds of the main issues that would subsequently constitute its most controversial and criticized inconveniences. Later on, these inconveniences would themselves emerge as the driving aspects of an urging reform movement to address the negative effects of the model, such as the formation of monopolies in the sector, the inaccuracy of remuneration schemes frequently based on unclear estimation of content use and lacking transparency to rightsholders, and, more recently, territorial limitations. As an underlying factor in all the reform initiative, the everlasting problem of balance between creators' rights, the legitimate interests of the industry that explores the activity, and the various other freedoms and protected fundamental values such as access to culture and science, expression, speech, initiative and so forth, to which a specific topic of this study has been previously dedicated.

Therefore, it can be said that before stronger regulation mechanisms took the floor, original functions of collective management organizations basically consisted in the centralization of the legal and commercial representation of holders of copyrights so as to provide their proper remuneration. The intermediation would be remunerated with a fraction of the collected fees, and the activity should be conducted such as to allow transactions costs to lower, efficiency to be improved, maximization of profits to be attained, copyright claims to be avoided or controlled, and the use of protected creation to be duly monitored for the enforcement of applicable legal remedies.[7]

---

[7] The Collective Management of Rights in Europe. The Quest for Efficiency. KEA European Affairs. July 2006. http://www.keanet.eu/report/collectivemanpdffinal.pdf.

4.2 Controversial Issues in the Context of Collective Rights Management

None of the previously mentioned imperfections in the system of collective management of creators' and artists' rights have been properly tackled after over two centuries of its designing and adoption, even after the whole new reality of digital networked collaborative technologies hit the scene. Notwithstanding some minor adjustments and in spite of some rather isolated and insufficient attempts of the sector to assimilate the impacts of sociodigitization, all of them remain causes of tension that has been building among stakeholders in the environment, and all of them are aspects addressed by the current reform initiatives.

4.2.1 Competition Issues

One of these points of criticism has always been the fact that the exclusivity rights that collective management organizations intermediate constituted a factual, when not legal monopoly, usually exempted from antimonopoly provisions but directly affecting competition, and as such unlikely to be naturally willing to adapt, comprehend, or evolve according to market needs and demands. Apart from objective legal competition concerns of abuse and dominance, this also draws economic auspices of mid- or long-term inefficiency.

In the European Union the issue has already been the object of extensive debate. Long before the entry into force of the new Directive 2014/26/EU on Collective Rights Management, monopolistic abuse of collecting societies has been discussed before the European Court of Justice. In *GVL v. Commission,* the Court decided that a collecting society in a position of a de facto monopoly to provide services indistinctly but who refuses the provision of these services to those who "do not come within a certain category of persons defined by the undertaking on the basis of nationality or residence must be regarded as an abuse of a dominant position."[8] In *Tournier*[9] the Court held that a copyright management society that happens to be in a dominant position "imposes unfair trading conditions where the royalties which it charges to discothèques are appreciably higher than those charged in other Member States, the rates being compared on a consistent basis", unless objective grounds of distinctions in copyright management systems between Member States are able to justify the charge differences. A Commission Recommendation on the management of online rights in musical works[10] from 2005, having recognized that a

---

[8] Case 7/82, GVL v. Commission, [1983] ECR 483, para 56.
[9] Case 395/87, Tournier, [1989] ECR 2521, paras 34–46; Joint Cases 110, 241 and 242/88, Lucazeau et al. v. SACEM, [1989] ECR 2811, paras 21–33.
[10] Commission Recommendation of 18 May 2005 on collective cross-border management of copyright and related rights for legitimate online music services.

4.2 Controversial Issues in the Context of Collective Rights Management

monopolistic organization in the licensing market might bring certain advantages for creators, concluded supporting the introduction of competition among collecting societies, under the argument that efforts to keep "administrative costs low and the quality of the services high are objectives that can be better guaranteed by competition among several collecting societies for right holders than by a monopoly."[11] Competition implications and effects in the context of the collective administration of rights over digital creative content was, for the mentioned reasons, a recurring issue during the reform debate.[12]

4.2.2 Transparency and Accountability

Then, there is transparency. A governance concern that seems to haunt the inner structures of collective rights management organizations all over the world. It has always been one of the strongest points of criticism directed to collecting societies, and rightfully so. The lack of general rules and principles regarding financial and administrative internal controls, public availability of information and accountability practices are unacceptable shortcomings in a society which is connected through networked and collaborative technologies. Worse, these tools seem to be perfectly sufficient to boost the content industry's results, but is still unable—or simply remains unemployed—to deliver the rightfully demanded level of transparency to holders of the managed revenue-generating rights. It is clear that the technological development described in earlier sections of this study impacted in the immaterial assets and interests that collecting organizations manage, but it is not less evident that this development should also reflect in the way these interests and assets themselves are managed, through established business enterprises. The first effect has been fully assimilated and the industry already uses every possible digital alternative to potentialize revenue. The associated effect in the governance of these organizations is yet to be felt.

Transparency is always a potentially positive outcome of the introduction of communication and information technologies in a given environment. The fact that data is treated electronically in the course of a certain activity means that this data is digitally stored, but also that it is subject to retrieval, when and if necessary. In other words, an adequate automation of a certain activity will allow the data that it deals with to be stored in a centralized and structured way and to be recovered automatically by individuals who wish to obtain relevant information from the stored data, efficiently, practically, and without the restrictions of old administrative controls and

---

[11] Drexl (2007).
[12] According to Hargreaves, another concern regarding competition law in the operation of collecting societies is that they manage what can be considered, at least for licensees, a *regulatory cost*, in a transaction where licensees do not enjoy the same protective framework, for example, of consumers in a similar circumstance (Hargreaves 2011, Prof Ian (May 2011). Digital Opportunity—A Review of Intellectual Property and Growth. UK Intellectual Property Office. p. 36).

bureaucratic paperwork. Prompt availability of good quality information is a good business practice whose offspring is a transparent undertaking. For authors and right holders, it is everything a collecting society is not, from negotiating contracts, through collecting revenue, organizing remuneration schemes, informing authors, monitoring different uses of their repertoire, managing its own administrative costs, making relevant information public or at least available to those with legitimate interests, until distributing results—including whatever else happens in between. Many of the collective management organizations currently active in the market "operate in a way that prevents rightsholders from accessing even the simplest financial information about societies, which proves particularly problematic with cross-border flows of royalties and other types of compensations."[13]

A more accountable administration of their rights has long been a fair demand from authors, creators, and other rightsholders, a worry shared by the European Court of Justice in the already mentioned *Tournier*[14] case, in which the ECJ held that CMOs should "undertake to increase transparency in regard to the payment charged to the users of phonograms in their repertoire, by separating the tariff that covers the royalty proper from the fee meant to cover the administration costs"[15] so as to allow justification grounds for charge differentiation to be examined under more objective criteria. Internal procedures in CMOs can vary to such an extent that it may happen that an author neither has any influence nor any proper access to the distribution model of the collecting society. To observe the simplest thing as if his remuneration is regular and correct, he at times may be confronted with unbearable burdens that make it impracticable only to demonstrate "the extent of use of his work(s)."[16] In extreme cases he may even see revenues that were collected not being distributed simply because CMOs did not care to search for the right holder and then redirected revenue to other authors or the CMO itself, being possible that this revenue very well be redirected even to finance events lobbying against the interests of artists' rights.[17]

Nevertheless, up until the coming into force of the new Directive, stakeholders would express nothing more than a broad, general feeling that the desirable degree of transparency would be achieved through very abstract, superficial, and undefined notions of good governance culture and practices. A report commissioned by the United Kingdom Prime Minister in the name of the Intellectual Property Office Report and independently conducted by Professor Ian Hargreaves in 2011 concluded that there would be significant increase in members' confidence in collective

---

[13] DIGITALEUROPE on the Draft Collective Rights Management Directive. Available at http://www.digitaleurope.org/DocumentDownload.aspx?Command=Core_Download&EntryId=552 Accessed p. 4.
[14] Case 395/87, Tournier, [1989] ECR 2521, paras 34–46.
[15] Axhamn and Guibault (2011).
[16] Ibid., p. 22.
[17] Berlin Music Week Panel—Copyright collecting societies at the European level—An evaluation—Berlin 2013, video, All2gethernow YouTube Channel, 13 September, viewed 5 May 2014, https://www.youtube.com/watch?v=dy9RLvulkwo.

management organizations should there be mandatory transparency, common standards and codes of good practice requirements for them to abide by, pointing out that "the British Copyright Council has put forward a set of principles for such codes. Consumer Focus has also suggested principles which these codes should incorporate."[18] An obligation to "publish clear, comparable tariffs for rights, enabling rights owners and users to choose which society to deal with based on the terms available" has also been suggested.[19] From a more concrete perspective, though, few insights and reflections.

From a technical perspective, this unclearness has always essentially been a data problem. The alternative that collecting societies have originally devised to charge for the use of the works they managed could not ignore an operational constraint of the time when the activity was put in place, namely, the fact that not every single use of every single protected work was reported, and that a widespread following of all the managed works in all possible venues where they could be used was unmanageable. Unable to count on precise information or accurate usage reports, and being impossible to follow rigorously the amount of times a certain work was used, the only way for organizations to ensure the remuneration they and their members were entitled to was to employ estimation methods. Charging, collecting and distributing revenue from the execution and broadcasting of an enormous amount of protected works are activities that have long been carried out almost exclusively admitting their use by a rough approximation, that could vary (still does) depending on each CMO's internal policies and business practices. These practices are still, as seen, not standardized. Together with blanket licenses and sampling methods that were further adopted, an extremely simple, comfortable and lucrative system was put in place by collective management organizations to generate revenue, less to the benefit of creators and artists, and much to their own.

It is true that this was once the only alternative to collect dividends in exchange for the use of creative works, and in this sense, a practical and inventive solution back then. But it is needless to say that it was, from scratch, a distorted system, inclined to facilitate the intermediation service to the most, minimizing efforts and risks for CMOs. It is also important to point out that since the sampling methods they apply are evidently not able to measure precisely the uses of the works of all artists, sample-based estimations tend to favor best ranked artists. At the end of the day, as a result, due to the inconveniences of an old-fashioned collecting system, which in the absence of a more operational form of charging for the use of intellectual work, is still based to a great extent on estimation, the collected revenue is hardly ever distributed in a fair, efficient way.

It has always been that way, but it need not continue to be so in a digital economy. The reason is simple: in a world of networked and collaborative technologies, in the era of analytics, when content flows one way, information flows back the other way around. It is in the very nature of electronic transactions the fact

---

[18] Hargreaves (2011).
[19] Ibid., p. 35.

that they are recordable, storable, identifiable, and traceable. And information is all that is needed to reconfigure this aspect of collecting rights so that it can respond better to the personal needs of rightholders.

Curiously, as time goes by and opportunities for new usages of creative content increase in number and scope, it does not become more difficult—in fact it becomes perfectly feasible—to track uses and put fair remuneration systems in place. The reason is exactly because the very same digital technologies covered in previous sections of this study that have contributed to the skyrocketing of the creative content market can be as well used as tools to enhance administrative controls and to automate managerial practices. De Werra[20] highlights that trend in Digital Rights Management (DRM) technologies and the risk they pose to the traditional roles of CMOs, since the mentioned technical mechanisms allow creators to "negotiate directly in an automatic processing system with their users and can also be paid directly. From this perspective, collecting societies would not have as vital a function as they used to have."[21]

Using technologies to address this issue can lead to redesign what artists have referred to as one of the cruelest means possible to distribute copyright revenue since technology to make it happen otherwise was available.[22] Tools and data are now accessible, and together with attitude and disposition to offer services that are fairer and that better reflect individual realities, that is all it takes. Initiatives such as Soundreef,[23] a service that offers remuneration based on extensive and accurate data gathering, processing, and aggregation seem to have realized that modern collecting societies are to be basically data processing societies, where technology must be at the service of efficiency for all stakeholders. There is no space whatsoever to question the evidence that the more members a collecting society gets to join it, the more bargaining power it achieves in the market, and the more it will be able to take advantage of the scale to reduce costs and maximize efficiency. But it is equally clear the demand from authors and creators that the role of their collecting intermediaries turn from simply growing, attracting more artists or just being stronger or more profitable, to effectively serving its members—and serving them accordingly.

Because of the relevance of all the aspects discussed in this section of the work, transparency and accountability of collective rights management organizations, a market whose figures can reach €6 billion every year in the European Union alone, €4.1 billion of which only in the recorded music industry,[24] has been another key issue in the reform debate that led to the new Collective Rights Management Directive.

---

[20] De Werra (2005).

[21] Ibid., pp. 121–122.

[22] Berlin Music Week Panel—Copyright collecting societies at the European level—An evaluation—Berlin 2013, video, All2gethernow YouTube Channel, 13 September, viewed 5 May 2014, https://www.youtube.com/watch?v=dy9RLvulkwo.

[23] See http://www.soundreef.com/en/. Accessed in August 1st, 2014.

[24] Artists will collect royalties no later than 9 months after the end of the financial year. "Spotifying" the EU's copyright laws by Dan Alexe, 26.11.2013—16:09. http://www.neurope.eu/article/%E2%80%9Cspotify-ing%E2%80%9C-eu%E2%80%98s-copyright-laws.

4.2.3 Multi-territorial Licensing

Finally, territorial limitations.

Multi-territorial licensing of online music is a core issue in the Digital Agenda for Europe.[25] In 2009 the Commission had already pointed out efforts to create cross-border licensing for musical works that had made European licensing platforms possible, "albeit limited to the digital reproduction rights involved in online dissemination."[26] By the time of the Digital Agenda Communication barriers that still hindered the free circulation of online content and services among EU Member States in the Internet were described in the document as *untenable*. It is indeed impossible to have a true and full single market in place and regularly functioning while "Europe remains a patchwork of national online markets and there are cases when Europeans are unable to buy copyright protected works or services electronically across a digital single market."[27] This results in a more restrict number of online music services available to the EU user. For that reason, facilitation of cross-border licensing figured among the measures that the institution believed could better contribute to fight the "persistent fragmentation stifling Europe's competitiveness in the digital economy."[28]

Professor Ian Hargreaves' expression of perplexity when touching the issue in the 2011 independent report already referred to in the course of this study speaks for itself when he notes that "24 years after the inauguration of the EU single market, it is surprising that a firm wishing to source or supply copyright content via a single channel across Europe is unable to do so."[29] If music is the kind of content one refers to, it is even more incomprehensible, for the simple fact that music is intrinsically multi-territorial. It has always been so. There is little point in thinking of an extensive multi-territorial legal system to discipline, for example, immovable property. It makes, however, plenty of sense to discipline immaterial creation in the current stage of technical development. Human expression is born borderless, and if for a long time this feature was not naturally highlighted it has only been because technical constraints did not render it possible. As soon as networked and collaborative technologies definitely brought economical and operational barriers down,

---

[25] Communication from the Commission to the European Parliament, the Council, the European Economic and Social Committee and the Committee of the Regions. A Digital Agenda for Europe /* COM/2010/0245 f/2 */.

[26] Creative Content in a European Digital Single Market: Challenges for the Future—A Reflection Document of DG INFSO and DG MARKT. 22 October 2009. http://ec.europa.eu/internal_market/consultations/docs/2009/content_online/reflection_paper%20web_en.pdf.

[27] Communication From The Commission To The European Parliament, The Council, The European Economic And Social Committee And The Committee Of The Regions. A Single Market for Intellectual Property Rights—Boosting creativity and innovation to provide economic growth, high quality jobs—and first class products and services in Europe Available at: http://ec.europa.eu/internal_market/copyright/docs/ipr_strategy/COM_2011_287_en.pdf.

[28] Ibid.

[29] Hargreaves (2011).

allowing artists to produce and distribute their work at reasonably lower costs and efforts, it has been precisely music, out of all the forms of expression subject to copyright provisions, that seemed to start benefitting more broadly, more directly and much faster than any other, from the conformation of the new market alternatives and demands. Music in a digital environment can be both produced and consumed easily, anywhere, and its final outcome speaks to the public regardless of time, nationality, physical support, or language.[30]

This is enough reason why it never sounded logical to continue compelling operators of creative digital content services to segment them on the basis of national boundaries anywhere in the world, but principally in a European Union that puts so much effort and trust in the integration effects of a Single Market. This imposes a burden of inefficiency and even anachronism over these businesses in a moment when it is exactly the dynamism and versatility of the global phenomenon in which they conduct their activities what gives them the opportunity to explore the new, make breakthroughs and keep the path of innovation and economic growth, while preserving cultural diversity and development.

Multi-territorial licensing and the critical integration dimension it raises in the search for an effective Single Market, as stated above, has been another component driving the collective rights management reform debate.

4.3 The Legal Framework of the Collective Rights Management (CRM) Directive

This topic revisits the same controversial issues that were addressed in the previous section, only this time from a post Directive 2014/26/EU point of view. The purpose is to follow the echo of the debate that preceded the entry into force of the Directive, and to examine how the critical arguments previously presented concerning competition, transparency, and multi-territorial licensing in the context of collective management organizations, aspects regarded as the core of the instrument,[31] contributed to the construction of the new framework. Directive 2014/26/EU on collective management of copyright and related rights and multi-territorial licensing of rights in musical works for online use in the internal market has been adopted on February 26, 2014, and published in the Official Journal of the European Union on March 20, 2014. It should be transposed in 24 months after its entry into force, according to its Article 43(1).[32]

---

[30] The Collective Management of Rights in Europe. The Quest for Efficiency. KEA European Affairs. July 2006. http://www.keanet.eu/report/collectivemanpdffinal.pdf.

[31] Commissioner Michel Barnier welcomes the trilogue agreement on collective rights management. European Commission—MEMO/13/955. 05/11/2013 http://europa.eu/rapid/press-release_MEMO-13-955_en.htm.

[32] Online music regulations, Youtube Channel of the Council of the EU. https://www.youtube.com/watch?v=bksKJL9BEfw&feature=c4-overview&list=UULPG_xkgSWeWnOhBsi-jxCA.

4.3 The Legal Framework of the Collective Rights Management (CRM) Directive

The Council of the European Union considers that the main objectives pursued by the Directive present proper alternatives to tackle the controversial issues that were raised in the previous topic of this work, long-lasting complaints that are sources of recurring tension in the context of collective management organizations. These objectives are to promote greater transparency and governance efficiency in the functioning of collective management organizations and to facilitate the granting of cross-border licensing of authors' rights in the online music market.[33] Competition concerns are implicit in both main objectives, through which the European administration hopes to use copyright as a tool both to bring additional incentive to innovative ideas and to reward creativity accordingly.

Broadly speaking, the Commission expects the Directive to redesign transparency practices in collective management organizations by strengthening their reporting obligations as well as by empowering rightsholders, thus providing them the conditions to exercise better control over the societies' activities and participating closer in their overall decision-making process. "Cases of mismanagement of rights revenue or long-delayed payments have shown that there is a need to improve the functioning of collective management organizations."[34]

The attempt to boost a cross-border licensing architecture is clearly a further effort to realize the European Union's potential in the digital market of music, though the provisions can and should also serve other segments of the industry. Subscription revenues of downloading or streaming music more than tripled to US $1.1 billion worldwide in the last 3 years,[35] and while the digital share of the market corresponds to almost 50 % of total spendings in music in the United States, the average figures in the EU do not yet reach 20 %.[36]

A number of position papers with contributions, favorable and contrary positions,[37] scholarly comments and the Commission guidelines, as well as additional

---

[33] Council of the European Union, Press Release. February 2014. Better access to online music—Collective management of copyright http://www.consilium.europa.eu/uedocs/cms_Data/docs/pressdata/en/intm/141081.pdf.

[34] Commissioner Michel Barnier welcomes the European Parliament vote on the Directive on collective rights management European Commission—MEMO/14/80 04/02/2014 http://europa.eu/rapid/press-release_MEMO-14-80_en.htm.

[35] Recording Industry in Numbers—an essential guide to global markets. International Federation of the Phonographic Industry. 1st April 2014. Press release. http://www.ifpi.org/news/IFPI-publishes-Recording-Industry-in-Numbers-2014.

[36] Commission Staff Working Document Impact Assessment. Accompanying the document Proposal for a Directive of the European Parliament and of the Council on collective management of copyright and related rights and multi-territorial licensing of rights in musical works for online uses in the internal market http://ec.europa.eu/internal_market/copyright/docs/management/impact_assesment-com-2012-3722_en.pdf.

[37] The Polish Parliament challenged the Draft Proposal it received, and decided almost unanimously that it did not comply with the principle of subsidiarity, or at least did not sufficiently clarify the reason why the envisaged objectives, particularly those in respect of the framework for multi-territorial licensing, could be more effectively attained on the EU level. Polish Parliament: proposed directive on collective rights management does not comply with principle of subsidiarity, 16.10.2012.

documents and reports used in the process of framing the new legal infrastructure for collecting societies will aid in the task of conducting this preliminary critical analysis of the adopted text—an analysis which is obviously restricted to the issues which are in the narrow scope of this study.

4.3.1 Competition Issues

Recovering the aspects that were faced in the previous topic, where this issue was analyzed in the context prior to the entry into force of Directive 2014/26/EU, it is necessary to say that competition concerns are most probably the issues with less objective, less explicit measures in this particular instrument, which by no means imply that they are not relevant, have been set aside, overridden, or not considered. Competition issues entail a broader, sometimes even covert approach, and whenever the economic component of a collecting management organization's activity is to raise compliance questions, like it was the case in *Tournier*,[38] competition fundamental principles and provisions undoubtedly apply, for they are at the base of the very concept of the internal market.

Moreover, earlier pieces of EU legislation, like the Information Society Directive,[39] already worked in fine-tuning the coordination of overlapping aspects of intellectual property rights and of the competition framework in the digital environment. The Information Society Directive proclaims, for example, that harmonization in both these fields contributes to achieve the objective of preventing distortion in the internal market,[40] that the investments in content provision and information technology that are sheltered by a solid system of protection of intellectual property rights lead to foster competitiveness,[41] that the digital environment requires collecting societies to achieve a higher level of rationalization and transparency so as to comply with competition rules,[42] whereas Article 9 determines more than the coexistence, the interaction between the system of the Directive and provisions of unfair competition.

Nevertheless, the newborn Directive 2014/26/EU reaffirms these ties, submitting agreements among collective management organizations to strict compliance with

---

(Footnote 37 continued)
http://kluwercopyrightblog.com/2012/10/16/the-polish-parliament-thinks-the-proposed-directive-on-collective-rights-management-does-not-comply-with-the-principle-of-subsidiarity/.

[38] Case 395/87, Tournier, [1989] ECR 2521, paras 34–46.

[39] Directive 2001/29/EC of the European Parliament and of the Council of 22 May 2001 on the harmonization of certain aspects of copyright and related rights in the information society.

[40] Ibid., Recital (1).

[41] Ibid., Recital (4).

[42] Ibid., Recital (17).

4.3 The Legal Framework of the Collective Rights Management (CRM) Directive

the competition rules laid down by Articles 101 and 102 TFEU,[43] and stating, further on, that the provision of individualized licenses for innovative online services should also comply with competition law.

Directive 2014/26/EU raises, however, some express competition concerns, as the one of Article 32, a derogation aimed at broadcast companies through which, unlike other activities, these undertakings are exempted from clearing rights on a multi-territorial basis to make their broadcasts available online, whether it be simultaneously with or after their initial broadcast. The given reason is because such uses are regarded as ancillary and are already covered by the license granted by collecting societies to broadcasting companies through what the Commission justified as "voluntary aggregation of the required rights in the local collective management organizations."[44] *Cable Europe*[45] required clarification of the originally proposed text, while in a Position Paper *PRS for Music* challenged the provision as distorting natural competition conditions, once in circumstances "Where broadcasters sell on demand audiovisual content they are in competition with commercial online audiovisual services companies. CMOs have to treat them equally for competition law reasons."[46] Article 32 was upheld and is in force.

Finally, the reasoning behind the establishment of tariffs is clearly also competition driven, as suggests terminology employed in Article 16. The provision states that tariffs and remuneration are to be reasonable and to reflect "the economic value of the use of the rights in trade." These are criteria that are subject to the scrutiny of national competition authorities, following rulings by the European Court of Justice in *Kanal 5 Ltd*,[47] where the Court decided that the establishment of prices should not be "excessive in relation to the value of the service provided" and "reasonable in relation to the economic value of the service provided", and also in *SENA*,[48] where the ECJ ruled that the fees charged by a collecting society "should reasonably relate to the economic value of the use of their respective repertoire."

---

[43] Directive 2014/26/EU on collective management of copyright and related rights and multi-territorial licensing of rights in musical works for online use in the internal market. Recital 11.

[44] European Commission—MEMO/14/79, 04/02/2014. http://europa.eu/rapid/press-release_MEMO-14-79_en.htm.

[45] Cable Europe Position Paper on the Commission's Proposal for a Directive on Collective Rights Management 25 February 2013, p. 7. http://icg.greens-efa.org/pipermail/hub/attachments/20130327/155f35f7/attachment-0018.pdf.

[46] Position Paper on the CRM Directive. PRS for Music, March 2013, http://www.prsformusic.com/SiteCollectionDocuments/CRM%20Directive%20PRS%20for%20Music%20Mar%202013%20English%20FINAL.pdf.

[47] Case C-52/07.

[48] Case C-245/00.

4.3.2 Transparency and Accountability

Then, again, there's transparency. In the corresponding topic of the previous section the vulnerabilities associated with the lack of an adequate level of transparency in the operation of collecting societies were analyzed from the perspective of a moment prior to the entry into force of Directive 2014/26/EU. This unsatisfactory level of transparency has been by far the source of most of the fierce criticism, and even to the considerable discredit the activity has been facing before the public opinion. Causes, as already mentioned, are old-fashioned, outdated, unclear, and most of the times unfair methods of collecting and distributing revenue with its members, extremely poor governance practices, little or virtually no information available to the public, members, and other legitimate interested parts, in addition to a number of obscure transactions. Bearable limits are at times completely ignored, with the discovery, for instance, of situations in which not only collected money is not rightfully and timely distributed, it is also employed in risk investments about which rightsholders, needless to say, have never been consulted. "The commission says an Italian collecting society in 2008 lost €35 million in a "debt instrument" with the failed investment bank Lehman Brothers"[49] and it seems the case is not the only one.[50]

Unlike the vague discourse of better practices and the abstract recommendations to which criticism was usually limited prior to the proposal and adoption of Directive 2014/26/EU, concrete provisions designed to tie business administration, financial controls and overall institutional governance together have now been introduced, are available and shall be enforced over the activity of collecting rights' revenue.

Chapter 5 of the Directive—Articles 18–22—is specific on *Transparency and Reporting*. In spite of that, interrelated instructions are dispersed, spread all the way through the text, an evidence that transparency, more than a worry to be addressed by one mere legal command, functions as an inspirational value of the Directive, through which European institutions hope that a business activity which is fundamental in a modern economy, and mainly in this delicate moment of crisis, opens new horizons and reaches more suitable efficiency levels to face the challenges with which it is constantly confronted.

Article 18 lays down rules on the provision of Information to *rightsholders on the management of their rights,* and determines that CMOs make available, at least once a year, information on identification and contact details (a), attributed revenue in the period (b), separated by category, if it is the case (c), and with the indication of period of use (d), deductions from management fees (e) or from any other reason (f), and any outstanding rights revenue (g). It is certainly the basic information for

---

[49] Europe Moves to Aid Digital Music Industry By Eric Pfanner Published: July 10, 2012. http://www.nytimes.com/2012/07/11/business/global/europe-moves-to-aid-digital-music-industry.html?_r=0.

[50] DutchNews.Nl. Music rights society loses on investments, Tuesday 26 May 2009. See more at: http://www.dutchnews.nl/news/archives/2009/05/music_rights_society_loses_on.php#sthash.6s7mN7FI.dpuf.

4.3 The Legal Framework of the Collective Rights Management (CRM) Directive

any economic transaction to develop under minimum professional conditions, but it is definitely more information than authors have ever had access—objective enforceable access—to.

In Article 19, rules turn themselves to *Information provided to other collective management organizations on the management of rights under representation agreements*, and establishes the obligation of providing, again not less than once a year, information on the revenue attributed for the rights a CMO manages under representation agreement, strictly discriminated per category of rights and per type of use, as well as information on outstanding revenue (a), deduction from management fees (b), or for any other source or purpose (c) and licenses granted or refused concerning rights under the representation agreement (d). A good governance practice is also established concerning the obligation of the CMO of informing partner CMOs of decisions by the general assembly that impact the management of the rights under an eventual representation agreement they have in place (e).

In the *chapeau*, an apparently unpretentious novelty sets the stage for the most promising trend in the Directive: the duty to observe that the *information* that Article 19 refers to shall also be compulsorily available *by electronic means* is a clear sign that policy makers have understood that the restructuring of the business practices of the sector demands a deeper cultural shift. Yes, there has be policy and yes, there has to be law, but success in desired changes and in the implementation of a new transparency paradigm in the sector will strongly depend upon the adequate use and adoption of information and communication technologies. It is the most promising trend of the instrument, albeit not an aim in itself, but a tool that serves straight purposes of the Directive, like the development of reliable multi-territorial licensing of online content and monitoring compliance with competition law, to name a few.

It is not that the times of absolutely personalized services between authors and collecting societies have come to all. Authors who need extremely individualized administration of their rights will still have to search and pay the higher cost of special services, should they feel this is the most suitable alternative to their needs. But technology, the same force that caused a revolution and boosted the production and use of content, is now in a legal position to give its share of contribution in enhancing the intermediation services inside the industry, helping distribute its results to creators in a manner which is at least fairer and definitively more tailored.

Basic estimation algorithms for collecting and distributing revenue no longer respond to the expectations of artists—the largest share of them—that live in the age of analytics and that are fully aware that available technologies allow collecting societies to do much better than they have historically done. Born digital[51] authors and creators urge the interaction with the administrators of their rights to reflect and principally to incorporate the dynamics of a networked and collaborative reality,

---

[51] Palfrey and Gasser have established as a criteria that this term relates to people who were born after 1980, when collaborative digital technologies were not yet in its full force. "They all have access to networked digital technologies. And they all have the skills to use those technologies." (Palfrey and Gasser 2008, Introduction, p. 1).

and require intermediation services "with the institutional transparency of GNU/ Linux and the analytic efficiency of Google."[52]

This is especially true in the case of the online music industry that operates a very large scale and where uses are significantly reported, illegal uses being out of the scope of this study. Service providers process millions of lines of data, billions of streaming and download transactions, all of which in a scenario with a huge number of works and rightsholders involved. Manual processing is impracticable, and it is evident that without accurate databases and strong processing capabilities, these complex processes will not be properly automated, and although more alternatives and options can be offered in the market, "the processing of those uses would not be economically viable."[53]

It seems that first important steps have been taken. Policy makers have unquestionably understood that transforming the profile of collecting management organizations requires them "the capacity to appropriately and accurately handle data electronically."[54] This will demand investment in appropriate information and communication equipment and data processing infrastructure to manage the large, dynamic electronic databases that will be at the heart of the service. Ultimately, a modern collecting society, as argued in the corresponding topic of the last section of this work, is to be a data processing society.

Still in the Chapter specifically dedicated to *Transparency and Reporting,* Article 20 sets rules for the serving of information upon request, not only reinforcing that electronic communication is mandatory, but also that this provision of information should happen *without undue delay.* An extensive, though not exhaustive description of the information that should be disclosed to the public is presented under Article 21, from which it is possible to underline *standard licensing contracts and standard applicable tariffs, including discounts* (c), a list of persons in charge of the administration (d), general policies on fees (f) and deductions (g), complaint-handling and dispute resolution procedures (j), once again with the express compulsory duty to disclose the information and keep it up-to-date also in electronic form (2).

The last move in the specific Chapter 5, Article 22 institutes the obligation for the collecting society to elaborate and publish an *Annual transparency report*, within 8 months from the end of the previous financial year, that should be electronically and publicly available for at least 5 years, and that should contain (2) extensive information detailed in the Annex to the Directive, like *balance sheet or a statement of assets and liabilities, an income and expenditure account for the financial year and a cash flow statement,* Annex 1 (a).

---

[52] Brazil's copyright societies indicted for fraud, new law demands efficient, transparent collecting societies Cory Doctorow at 5:44 am Sun, Apr 29, 2012. http://boingboing.net/2012/04/29/brazils-copyright-societies.html.
[53] Ibid., p. 97.
[54] European Commission—MEMO/14/79, 04/02/2014.

4.3 The Legal Framework of the Collective Rights Management (CRM) Directive

Out of the specific *Transparency and Reporting* Chapter, as already mentioned, other provisions strengthen transparency practices, as the obligation imposed on a CMO *to communicate with its members by electronic means, including for the purpose of the exercise of their rights,* that is defined in Article 6(4), and the mechanisms of reporting the use of online works of Article 27(2), and of invoicing service providers of Article 27(3), both of which shall be offered through at least one method of electronic data exchange, automating the tasks, reducing duplication or inconsistency, and improving accuracy and timing of both reporting and invoicing.

Still concerning auditing and accountability, procedures laid down in Article 36 require Member States to designate competent authorities to monitor compliance with the Directives' commands (1). There is no need to designate dedicated supervisors for the related tasks, and certainly no obligation to set up an independent body, agency or to institute a separate national infrastructure like a national competition authority to monitor collective management organizations,[55] but the incumbents who will carry out the tasks *must have the power to impose appropriate sanctions or to take appropriate measures* (3) should they find that observed entities fail to comply.

The command of Article 13 states that the distribution of royalties shall be made within a stricter fixed period of 9 months, and the decisions concerning the use of revenue deemed nondistributable when a collecting society cannot find the right holder is explicitly submitted to the general assembly (5), provided that national law of the Member States on the statute of limitation of claims is observed.

The transparency problem has been building up for over a century in the structure of collecting management organizations all over the world, and in Europe in particular. Difficulties only seem to mount, and every day challenges do not seem to lessen, nor to become easier. By providing rules that will impose better practices in this field, Directive 2014/26/EU can give one of its most significant contributions to render the activity of online offer of content better prepared to face the dynamics and the pitfalls of a network society.

4.3.3 Multi-territorial Licensing

The objective of the 10 Articles of Title III of Directive 2014/26/EU is to bring down the barriers described in the corresponding topic of the previous section of this work, so that online creative content can be available faster, cheaper and on a wider basis, with more choices for consumers, promoting innovation, encouraging experiences for new services, improving present conditions, and opening new horizons for existing services and rightsholders, all of which will contribute to move the context in the EU closer to the ideal of a fully-implemented and functioning Digital Single Market.

---

[55] This was suggested in a number of position papers.

It is neither the first attempt, nor the first developments in this direction. In a previous recommendation, back in 2005,[56] the European Commission had already tried to structure an adequate framework for the management of online music rights, envisaging EU-wide licensing. In spite of that, further on, in 2008, the Commission prohibited 24 collecting societies in Europe from offering services to artists or content users outside their domestic territory over the argument that the contracts they celebrated among themselves contained membership and exclusivity clauses. The Commission also identified a concerted practice among investigated societies,[57] by which they restricted the right to grant licenses relating to their own repertoire in the territory of each other. Most societies involved, and also the International Confederation of Societies of Authors and Composers, brought an action before the European Court of Justice, where the Commission's decision concerning the recognition of the concerted practice was overturned due to lack of sufficient evidence, but upheld regarding the prohibition of membership and exclusivity clauses.[58] The Commission encouraged cross-border licensing efforts, recognized their importance, but was at the same time fighting what it considered to be inappropriate approaches or illegal initiatives. The online music licensing environment evidently needed a clearer framework to address multi-territoriality.

It is a new opportunity that comes at a cost. Arguments developed in the last topic lead to the conclusion that there is no possible economic viability in services that provide online creative content if they are not offered in a strongly data processing supported environment. It is simply not possible to manually handle the amount of data, monitor the amount of transactions, or perform the amount of operational and administrative controls that such an activity requires. It is taking this reasoning into consideration that Articles 23 and 24 of the new Directive restrict the new multi-territorial economic operation to those collective management organizations that comply with the requirements laid down in the directive, that is to say, that are able to process electronically the necessary data "for the administration of such licenses, including for the purposes of identifying the repertoire and monitoring its use, invoicing users, collecting rights revenue and distributing amounts due to rightsholders,"[59] what also implies the need to identify musical works,[60] in whole or in part, the rights and the corresponding rightsholders for each

---

[56] Music copyright: Commission recommendation on management of online rights in musical works European Commission—IP/05/1261 12/10/2005. Press release. http://europa.eu/rapid/press-release_IP-05-1261_en.htm?locale=en.

[57] Commission Decision relating to a proceeding under Article 81 of the EC Treaty and Article 53 of the EEA Agreement (Case COMP/C2/38.698—CISAC).

[58] Press release no. 43/13, General Court of the European Union. The General Court partially annuls the Commission decision finding anticompetitive conduct on the part of copyright collecting societies. http://curia.europa.eu/jcms/upload/docs/application/pdf/2013-04/cp130043en.pdf.

[59] Directive 2014/26/EU. Article 24(1).

[60] Article 24(1)(a).

4.3 The Legal Framework of the Collective Rights Management (CRM) Directive

of these works[61] using, when possible, industry identification standards,[62] and to resolve, timely and efficiently, data inconsistencies.[63]

Transparency principles are reinforced in Article 25, regulated in a way that they also apply to the provision by CMOs of information upon request concerning works represented, their rights and scope and the covered territories, always stressing the mandatory duty to ensure electronic communication. The directive imposes practices to ensure accuracy of the repertoire information in Article 26, reporting and invoicing in Article 27, and payments in Article 28, always stressing that there should be always at least one electronic manner to exchange data for these purposes, preferably abiding by "voluntary industry standards or practices developed at international or Union level."[64] The objective is evidently to promote the higher possible standard of interoperability among different systems.

Through Article 29, the Directive imposes representation agreements for multi-territorial licensing to be celebrated without exclusivity clauses,[65] to avoid the restriction of alternatives both for content users that will search for this new kind of arrangement, and for collective management organizations that do not intend to meet the somewhat burdensome necessary requirements to offer the service of multi-territorial licensing, but which have chosen to search for a partner society to manage their repertoire on a multi-territorial basis. This is a situation that raises competition and nondiscrimination concerns. If this request occurs, the envisaged partner may not refuse the representation service if it is already representing or has offered to represent the repertoire of another collective management organization for the same purposes.[66] In this case, it shall manage the represented repertoire applying the same conditions under which it manages its own repertoire (3), including it in all its offers to online service providers (4) and at reasonable fees (5).

The Directive takes into account that compliance with the multi-territorial licensing requirements can be costly, and that it can even turn out to be a complex and time-taking business decision. Artists who believe they could benefit from multi-territorial licensing, on the other hand, may not be indefinitely attached to a collecting society which cannot (or just will not) meet the compliance requirements to offer such licenses. The transition clause of Article 31 establishes a *no lock* mechanism for the work with a checkpoint in 2017. By that time, such authors who do not yet have access to multi-territorial treatment can withdraw from the organization only the specific rights that are necessary to explore multi-territorial licensing, entrusting some other entity for that purpose or just deciding to do it themselves, all with the possibility of leaving the original collecting society which

---

[61] Article 24(1)(b).
[62] Article 24(1)(c).
[63] Article 24(1)(d).
[64] Article 27(2).
[65] Recital 44.
[66] Article 30.

does not operate multi-territorial licensing in charge of granting ordinary licenses for a single territory.

Finally, the derogation concerning broadcasters contained in Article 32 and the criticism it raised during the discussions of the Directive, as well as the justification of the Commission to uphold it[67] are issues that have already been previously discussed in topic 4.4.1.[68]

A very brief comment on jurisdiction as a last word regarding aspects of multi-territoriality.

If territoriality only is already a pervasive notion in international litigation that acquires an even additional importance in intellectual property matters,[69] what could be said about this pervasive notion, with additional importance going online and spreading its effects everywhere? Now, make a ubiquitous activity multi-territorial, so that both its normal developments and eventually its related wrongdoings are also multi-territorial and ubiquitous, and we definitely have a rich and mind-provoking scenario for the discussion of jurisdictional issues, cross-border remedies and litigation in cases concerning the new multi-licensing legal framework. As if that were not enough, we could still add other even more sophisticated components, and consider the perspective that the very concept of territoriality has changed,[70] or wander if and where procedural efficiency should prevail over the idea of territoriality.[71]

---

[67] The Directive was adopted with separate statements from Germany and The Netherlands, to clarify that the expert groups referred in Article 41 were not covered in the Framework Agreement on relations between the European Parliament and the European Commission (OJ L 304/47) and to "underline that the Treaty on the European Union, nor the Treaty on the Functioning of the European Union, foresee in a role for the European Parliament with regard to tasks relating to the application of directives and regulations." Slovenia expressed reservations in respect to the negative potential aspects of excessive fragmentation of repertoires managed by several organizations as a consequence of the cross-border alternatives, in respect to alleged lack of clarification or the responsibilities of relevant compliance authorities, and also that the lack of uniformity in the EU regarding this issue could undermine enforcement. Latvia issued a statement concerning inconsistent use of legal terminology in the translated version of Latvian language, that could lead to ambiguity and disruption of parallelism amongst different language versions of the text. Finally, Poland's statement expressed the worries that multi-territorial licensing could end up reinforcing the power of the collecting societies that represented "the most popular anglo-american repertoire", which, according to the statement, could "be detrimental to the repertoires with limited linguistic presence in the EU and would cause harm to the principle of safeguarding cultural diversity". Interinstitutional File: 2012/0180 (COD) Statement by the Republic of Poland. http://register.consilium.europa.eu/doc/srv?l=EN&f=ST%206434%202014%20ADD%201.

[68] The exact text of Article 32 states that the provisions "shall not apply to collective management organisations when they grant, on the basis of the voluntary aggregation of the required rights, in compliance with the competition rules under Articles 101 and 102 TFEU, a multi-territorial licence for the online rights in musical works required by a broadcaster to communicate or make available to the public its radio or television programmes simultaneously with or after their initial broadcast as well as any online material, including previews, produced by or for the broadcaster which is ancillary to the initial broadcast of its radio or television programme."

[69] Nuyts and Nikitas (2008).

[70] Nikitas (2007), p. 307.

[71] Ibid.

The Directive does not touch that quicksand, and that being the case, those issues fall out of the scope of this analysis. Article 34 merely determines that Member States should ensure effective alternative resolution procedures for certain kinds of enumerated disputes concerning all parts potentially involved, whereas Article 35 (2) simply reaffirms the application of rules on private international law relating to the conflict of laws and the jurisdiction of courts,[72] and the consequent rights of the parts to seek judicial protection, should they feel necessary or appropriate.

4.4 Creators X Creative Industry—Are We Speaking the Same Language?

The idea of art as an instrument to a fairer distribution of wealth could not be more romantic, and poetic. Seductive, in fact. The surprising thing is that digital technologies in a network society connected by collaborative tools can prove this idea to have economic grounds—and adequate legislation can provide a framework where it also has legal viability.

Intellectual Property had already found an interesting new channel of operation and distribution of content through the very first information technology mechanisms aforementioned. They already presented enough alternatives to raise challenging concerns to the industry. But it is only starting from the following social configuration this study refers to, namely, a *network society*, where not only information or communication, strictly speaking, but *interaction* was given floor, when the emission pole of information[73] was liberated, allowing users not only to consume, as traditionally, but also, for the first time in history, to produce and interfere with the information now flowing online, that the electronic atmosphere speeds its way as one of the potentially most democratic, borderless environment the world has ever witnessed. To the generation that is rising from this shift, the notion of media, to give an example, has never been perceived within the conventional sense of something relating to a material, physical support (*chorpus mechanicum*), subject to individual and exclusive appropriation. It is a generation that is not even familiar with the paradigm of materiality. This is huge.

On the other side, a stable and fully-implemented and functioning digital and Internet-based industry has in a solid and efficient Single Digital Market an incredible opportunity of expansion alternatives, both for periods of normality and for situations of crisis. Formerly unseen social possibilities derived from technological conditions have attracted millions to the ecosystems of the most different social media tools, and these tools are nowadays recognized as an essential, strategical channel for interaction, in general, and for cultural creation and sharing of

---

[72] Recital 56.
[73] Lemos (2007), p. 20.

ideas, in particular. It is a context that has taken social media to be perceived as an environment to promote, assure and fight for this new important components of the freedom of expression: the powers to access, create, and distribute.

Finally, the economic activity that exploits the result of human creation is absolutely legitimate. It plays a very important role in raising the value of art and artists and can play an even more important role with the enforcement of the legal instruments discussed here, a well deserved legal protection for an activity with a clearly recognizable economic dimension.

A new technical reality, providing expansion of interaction upon more democratic grounds, with significant economic repercussion, all protected by legal instruments which have to be constructed envisaging the promotion of creation opportunities and of the organized activity itself. Creators and the creative industry are key players in this phenomena, their activities, their interests, and their interactions directly feel the effects mentioned above, but the fact is that they have always been treated essentially differently and although creative industries have always enjoyed relatively comfortable levels of legal protection, creators definitely have not. This is a difference which legislation and the public debate have not been adequately addressing or taking account of. By implementing express and objective compliance mechanisms and enhancing controls regarding the monitoring of compliance, the new framework could be contributing to level this playing field and reducing this historical distortion.

A legal framework where general compliance is more strongly enforced and more easily monitored and attainable may not make a huge difference to high-end artists and high performance businesses, for whom negotiations, contracts, and transactions with the ones who manage their interests are more often than not individualized. Transparency, accountability, enforcement, or compensation in case of breaches is a problem they are perfectly used to facing with the significant amount and quality of resources (market, communication, legal, economic, strategic, musical, etc.) that they have at hand. The creative industry is essentially a business—and commonly big business—which only happens to be developed using the human expression as its main input.

But for the average individual creator, away from large and professional structures, someone that can hardly access the necessary resources to enforce his rights or monitor the uses of his work, a framework that imposes clear compliance obligations and improves monitoring instruments can have a great impact on how results of his work return to him. Opposing the logic of creative enterprises, the work of the average artist is essentially human expression, which happens to have economic potential. It is an inversion of approach that has historically put creators and creative industries in completely different positions considering the legal protection at their reach. New mechanisms can start to tell a fairer story.

This is not an objective which is expressly stated in the new Directive, although it is possible to imagine it as a long-term side effect of the reform. It can be remarkably relevant, not only for artists and other rightsholders, but for the activity as a whole. Why? It is a question of scale and revenue distribution. Big businesses transact huge amounts of money, which is concentrated in the hands of a few, revenue that has always been and will continue to be closely and professionally kept track of and that for this reason already reaches rightsholders. The average individual creator is hundreds of times more numerous, technology allows this profile to grow, produce and experience more by the day, but at times he did not have the resources to seek for the revenue to which he is entitled. The potential effect of the new legal structure in this scenario is obvious. Whether it be from a sustainable development point of view, from a macroeconomic perspective, from an innovation fostering or from a social justice standpoint, it can be much more interesting to have in place a legal framework that will favor the rightful distribution of the revenue collected in the names of the artists, allowing more artists to receive the proper return from their creative activity, encouraging diversity, respecting and promoting a historically neglected alternative economic activity, than to have one that takes even better care of fewer fortunes that would reach their destination anyway—even if, at the end of the day, there's no essential aesthetic difference in the artistic output that originates from individual creators and from big players from the creative industry.

The new European framework creates the conditions for distribution, on this grounds, to become a reality.

References

Axhamn J, Guibault L (2011) Cross-border extended collective licensing: a solution to online dissemination of Europe's cultural heritage?—Final report prepared for EuropeanaConnect. Instituut voor Informatierecht, Universiteit van Amsterdam, Amsterdam, The Netherlands, Aug 2011

Berlin music week panel—copyright collecting societies at the European level—an evaluation—Berlin 2013, video, Alltogethernow YouTube Channel, 13 September, viewed 5 May 2014. https://www.youtube.com/watch?v=dy9RLvulkwo

Collective Management in Reprography, World Intellectual Property Organization (WIPO) and the International, 2004 Federation of Reproduction Rights Organisations (IFRRO). http://www.ifrro.org/upload/documents/wipo_ifrro_collective_management.pdf

Commission staff working document impact assessment accompanying the document proposal for a directive of the European Parliament and of the Council on collective management of copyright and related rights and multi-territorial licensing of rights in musical works for online uses in the internal market. http://ec.europa.eu/internal_market/copyright/docs/management/impact_assesment-com-2012-3722_en.pdf

Communication from the commission to the European Parliament, the council, the European economic and social committee and the committee of the regions. A single market for intellectual property rights—boosting creativity and innovation to provide economic growth, high quality jobs—and first class products and services in Europe. http://ec.europa.eu/internal_market/copyright/docs/ipr_strategy/COM_2011_287_en.pdf

Creative content in a European digital single market: challenges for the future—a reflection document of DG INFSO and DG MARKT. http://ec.europa.eu/internal_market/consultations/docs/2009/content_online/reflection_paper%20web_en.pdf. Accessed 22 Oct 2009

De Werra J (2005) Access control or freedom of access. In: Digital rights management: the end of collecting societies? Berne/New York/Brusells/Athens 2005, pp 111–122

Digital Europe on the draft collective rights management directive. http://www.digitaleurope.org/DocumentDownload.aspx?Command=Core_Download&EntryId=552. Accessed 15 March 2015

Directive 2001/29/EC of the European Parliament and of the Council of 22 May 2001 on the harmonisation of certain aspects of copyright and related rights in the information society

Directive 2001/29/EC on the harmonisation of certain aspects of copyright and related rights in the information society

Directive 2014/26/EU on collective management of copyright and related rights and multi-territorial licensing of rights in musical works for online use in the internal market

Drexl J (2007) Collecting societies and competition law. http://www.ip.mpg.de/shared/data/pdf/drexl_-_crmos_and_competition.pdf

European Commission (2006) Copyright Levies in a Converging World. Stakeholder Consultation, DG MARKT

Europe moves to aid digital music industry By Eric Pfanner. http://www.nytimes.com/2012/07/11/business/global/europe-moves-to-aid-digital-music-industry.html?_r=0. Accessed 10 July 2012

Hargreaves I (2011) Digital opportunity—a review of intellectual property and growth

Inter Institutional File: 2012/0180 (COD) Statement by the Republic of Poland. http://register.consilium.europa.eu/doc/srv?l=EN&f=ST%206434%202014%20ADD%201

Kroes N (2014)Completing the EU digital market must be top priority for the next Commission. Ecommerce Europe YouTube Channel. Global Ecommerce Summit 2014 in Barcelona, viewed 14 May 2014. https://www.youtube.com/watch?v=EhFlx5MjwO4

Lemos (2007) Ciberespaço e tecnologias móveis: processos de territorialização e desterritorialização na cibercultura. In: MÉDOLA, Ana Silvia; ARAÚJO, Denise; BRUNO, Fernanda (Org.). Imagem, visibilidade e cultura midiática. Porto Alegre: Sulina, 2007

Nikitas (2007) Concluding remarks: territoriality, international governance and cross-border litigation of intellectual property claims. In: Nuyts A, Hatzimihail N, Szychowska K (eds) International litigation in intellectual property and information technology. Kluwer, New York, pp 303–308. http://ssrn.com/abstract=2238483

Nuyts A, Hatzimihail N (2008) Concluding remarks: territoriality, international governance and cross-border litigation of intellectual property claims. In: Nuyts A, Hatzimihail N, Szychowska K (eds) International litigation in intellectual property and information technology. Kluwer, New York, pp 303–308. SSRN:http://ssrn.com/abstract=2238483

Online music regulations, Youtube channel of the council of the EU. https://www.youtube.com/watch?v=bksKJL9BEfw&feature=c4-overview&list=UULPG_xkgSWeWnOhBsi-jxCA

Palfrey J, Gasser U (2008) Born digital—understanding the first generation of digital natives. B. Books, New York

Polish Parliament: proposed directive on collective rights management does not comply with principle of subsidiarity16.10.2012. http://kluwercopyrightblog.com/2012/10/16/the-polish-parliament-thinks-the-proposed-directive-on-collective-rights-management-does-not-comply-with-the-principle-of-subsidiarity/

Recording industry in numbers—an essential guide to global markets. International Federation of the Phonographic Industry. 1st April 2014. Press release. http://www.ifpi.org/news/IFPI-publishes-Recording-Industry-in-Numbers-2014

The Collective Management of Rights in Europe. The Quest for Efficiency KEA European Affairs. July 2006. http://www.keanet.eu/report/collectivemanpdffinal.pdf

Chapter 5
Conclusion

Technologies have always been natural catalysts of change, but the digital technologies of our time have surely transformed social, cultural, and economic interaction faster and more deeply than it has ever happened in any society throughout history. The impact of collaboration tools in the activity of creating intellectual content transformed the way collective management organizations operate and current market requirements demand legal adaptation to face this new reality. Collecting societies are important players in the content industry, and a number of relevant issues are addressed in the ongoing redesigning process of the legal model in which they operate, many of which are not even superficially discussed in this work, like strictly illegal or non-commercial uses, exceptions or protection of cultural heritage, for this would exceed its scope as it was delimited, that is to say, issues of competition, transparency, and multi-territorial licensing of rights over online protected works that are collectively managed.

A whole new social architecture communicates, interacts, demands, produces, and distributes information and impacts on the exercise of creativity and on other general aspects of cultural expression and intellectual property issues. It surely has various repercussions in aspects of production of intellectual content. Wide sharing and collaboration possibilities that technologies introduce in the social interaction promote the creation of intellectual content from various perspectives. This new environment is a tool, not a fight or an object in itself, which people—the real protagonists of changes—should explore to reach their goals. It's a catalyst, not an aim.

Boosting access to online services and content is one of the strategic objectives established in the Digital Agenda for Europe, and modernization of the activity of collective management of artists' rights is an important component in attaining this objective. Transparency practices in these businesses have long been outdated and had recently crossed the boundaries of reasonable tolerance, with repeated reports of misuse of collected and undistributed revenue of artists' rights, while many creators did not receive enough, if at all, the revenue generated by the use of their works. Controls have to be improved, and it has to be done in such a way as to maintain the viability of the activity, making sure the costs of collecting and distributing still reasonably pays. Efficiency and agility are also crucial in a very dynamic market where saying a slow "yes" to a license may be equivalent to saying "no"—and missing an opportunity that is always to be cherished—in times of crisis or not. Finally, a model of online provision of content in the European Union that presents serious barriers for cross-border operations and access is certainly one to be reconsidered, because it fails to envisage and to pursue the objectives of a fully functioning Single Market, especially in a digital world, where barriers, including formal borders, do not naturally exist.

Directive 2014/26/EU is the first intervention of this magnitude the European Union experiences in the matter. Prior attempts did not respond accordingly, and the Directive now in force is in process of transposition by Member States. The concern of transparency is addressed through a number of measures covering accountability and reporting, disclosure of information to the public or interested parts, designation of national authorities to monitor compliance and receive infringement reports (although there has been criticism that these structures should be even stronger and more independent), but principally through the massive use of the available technological instruments that provide "enhanced capability to process large amounts of data, accurate identification of the works used by the service providers, fast invoicing to service providers and timely payment to right-holders".[1] Multi-territorial licensing is also addressed by a clearer framework on representation agreements, with rules on non-discrimination, non-exclusivity, and non-refusal. Collective management organizations that intend to operate these new alternative of cross-border licensing will have to comply with strict technical requirements, demonstrating they have put in place data management tools that are able to process electronically the necessary data for the administration of the licenses they contractually receive, including identification of the repertoire, monitoring use, invoicing users, collecting and distributing revenue to rightsholders, which, in its turn, includes the need to identify musical works, in whole or in part, the rights and the corresponding rightsholders for each of these works using, when possible, industry identification standards, and to resolve, timely and efficiently, data inconsistencies. Concerns that the Commission's approach to the issue was sectorial, and that it promoted insufficient harmonization of national law to deal with these circumstances on a EU Level were expressed by stakeholders, including some Member States.

The framework now in place addresses multi-territoriality for the future. Although the integration process under the idea of the Single Market is not a new one, this licensing alternative is a recently born technical reality. It was only made possible under the current scene in technological development, and thus can only look and direct its effects forward.

---

[1] European Commission—MEMO/14/79, 04/02/2014. http://europa.eu/rapid/press-release_MEMO-14-79_en.htm.

5 Conclusion

The attempt to increase transparency and improve governance practices, on the contrary, has an eye in the past. Serious incidents of misuse of revenue[2] have contributed to raise the already huge level of criticism that collective management organizations have received, not to mention the perplexity that emerges from the anachronistic contact of a new generation of born digital artists and these enterprises' current unsatisfactory and inefficient instruments of control, reporting and communication with members, artists, rightsholders and content users. The result is a serious, though perfectly comprehensible crisis of legitimacy and representation of the sector as a business. The Directive is a useful instrument available for collective societies to accomplish this objective of rebuilding their image and appear as undertakings that are willing and making efforts to work under proper levels of transparency and that fulfill a legitimate economic activity providing good, fair and tailored intermediation services, while contributing to the promotion of creation, opportunities and diversity.

Lastly, it is undoubtedly interesting to observe that the very same digital technologies that have contributed to the skyrocketing of the creative content market as production tools are now reintroduced in the sector, but this time used as instruments to enhance administrative controls and to automate managerial practices. It is possible that the market is, in fact, on the way to a consolidated global copyright database,[3] which would be the ultimate optimization of the model, after all, at the end of the day, as long as the online content market is concerned, non european territories also matter. Only if that were to be a concrete proposal, the European Union would have to face even greater obstacles than it starts facing now with the implementation efforts of the framework contained in the recently adopted Directive.

References

Directive 2014/26/EU on collective management of copyright and related rights and multi-territorial licensing of rights in musical works for online use in the internal market
Summary of CISAC's World Copyright Summit #3. Creating value in the digital economy. Panel by panel, speech by speech, Brussels, 7–8 June 2011. http://www.cisac.org/CisacPortal/initConsultDoc.do?idDoc=22436

---

[2] The Impact Assessment that the Commission used in the reform negotiations showed that in the EU CMSs collect more revenue than in any other region of the world. Much of this money, though, never get to the artists. "Only 27–45 % of collections is distributed in the year of collection, in some cases part of the income collected is never distributed at all. In 2010 major societies had accumulated € 3.6 billion that they owed to rightsholders."

[3] Summary of CISAC's World Copyright Summit #3 (2011).

Bibliography

Anon, Digital Europe—creating a European copyright system for the digital age. http://www.digitaleurope.org/Aboutus/Structure/WorkingGroups/DigitalEconomyPolicyGroup/Copyrightleviesgroup.aspx. Accessed 15 Dec 2013

Audretsch DB, Lehmann EE, Link AN, Starnecker A (2012) Technology transfer in a global economy. Springer, New York

Barnier M (2013) Digital Single Market: let's make reality match our vision! European Commission—SPEECH/13/476 28/05/2013. http://europa.eu/rapid/press-release_SPEECH-13-476_en.htm. Accessed 15 Dec 2013

Beck U (2002) La sociedad del riesgo: hacia una nueva modernidad. Ediciones Paidós Ibérica

Benkler Y (1998) Overcoming agoraphobia: building the commons of the digitally networked environment. Harvard J Law Technol 11:287–400

Case C-275/06 (2008) Productores de Música de España (Promusicae) v Telefónica de España SAU ECR I-271

Convention for the Protection of Industrial Property (1883) Paris. http://www.wipo.int/treaties/en/text.jsp?file_id=288514. Accessed 14 April 2014

Dean D, DiGrande S, Field D, Lundmark A, O'Day J, Pineda J, Zwillenberg P (2012) The Internet economy in the G-20. The $4.2 trillion growth opportunity. Boston Consulting Group. https://www.bcgperspectives.com/content/articles/media_entertainment_strategic_planning_4_2_trillion_opportunity_internet_economy_g20/. Accessed 19 March 2012

Depreeuw S, Brison F (2011) The variable scope of the exclusive economic rights in copyright: exploring the articulation of law and technology through the case of Web search engines. VUB, Brussel

Directive 2006/115/EC of the European Parliament and of the Council of 12 Dec 2006 on rental right and lending right and on certain rights related to copyright in the field of intellectual property

Drexl J Max Planck Institute for Intellectual Property and Competition Law comments on the Proposal Directive on CMOs. http://www.ip.mpg.de/files/pdf2/Max_Planck_Comments_Collective_Rights_Management.pdf

European Commission (2013) Licences for Europe: industry pledges solutions to make more content available in the Digital Single Market. http://europa.eu/rapid/press-release_IP-13-1072_en.htm?locale=en

European Commission (2013) Proposal for a Directive of the European Parliament and of the Council on collective management of copyright and related rights and multi-territorial licensing of rights in musical works for online uses in the internal market. http://ec.europa.eu/internal_market/copyright/docs/management/com-2012-3722_en.pdf

European Commission, The EU Single Market—management of copyright and related rights. http://ec.europa.eu/internal_market/copyright/management/index_en.htm#maincontentSec1

Gracz K On the role of copyright protection in the information society Anti-ACTA Protests in Poland as a lesson in participatory democracy. PhD candidate at the Department of Law, European University Institute, Florence

Handke C, Towse R (2007) Economics of copyright collecting societies (12 July 2008). Int Rev Intellect Prop Compet Law 38(8):937–957. SSRN:http://ssrn.com/abstract=1159085 or http://dx.doi.org/10.2139/ssrn.1159085

Intellectual Property Office, UK (2011) Private copying and fair compensation: an empirical study of copyright levies in Europe

Kahin B, Varian HR (2000) Internet publishing and beyond: the economics of digital information and intellectual property. MIT Press, Cambridge

Kretschmer M (2011) Private copying and fair compensation: an empirical study of copyright levies in Europe (1 Oct 2011). An independent report commissioned by the UK Intellectual Property Office. ISBN:978-1-908908-11-7. SSRN:http://ssrn.com/abstract=2063809

Le Figaro Guerre des taxis : Uber partiellement interdit dans les rues de BruxellesChloé Woitier Publié le 16/04/2014 à 10:42. http://www.lefigaro.fr/secteur/high-tech/2014/04/16/01007-20140416ARTFIG00100-guerre-des-taxis-uber-partiellement-interdit-dans-les-rues-de-bruxelles.php

Lessig L (2001) The future of ideas: the fate of the commons in a connected world. Random House

Lessig L (2004) Free culture: how big media uses technology and the law to lock down culture and control creativity. Penguin Press

Lessig L, Zittrain J, Nesson CR, Fisher WW, Benkler Y (2002) Internet law. Foundation Press

Macnab LC, Faull J (2010) The compatibility of EU digital rights management legislation with EU competition law. VUB, Brussel

Morozov E (2009) The net delusion

Mylly T Constitutional functions of the EU's intellectual property treaties. http://www.utu.fi/en/units/law/faculty/faculty-staff/Documents/constitutional_aspects_of_ip_treaties.pdf

Mylly T (2012) Intellectual property and competition law in the information society. In: Geiger C (ed) Constructing European intellectual property. Achievements and new perspectives. Edward Elgar. http://www.utu.fi/en/units/law/faculty/faculty-staff/Documents/intellectual_property_and_competition_law_in_the_information_society.pdf

Postigo H (2012) The digital rights movement: the role of technology in subverting digital copyright. MIT Press, Cambridge

Solove D (2004) The digital person—technology and privacy in the informations age. New York University Press

Song Summit (2012) Content, competition, collecting societies and crystal balls—Sidney 2012, video, Song Summit's YouTube Channel, 16 Aug 2012, viewed 14 May 2014. https://www.youtube.com/watch?v=X4ZBz1_nt_Y

Stokes S (2014) Digital copyright: law and practice, 4th edn. Hart, Oxford

Tridente A (2009) Direito Autoral – Paradoxos e Contribuições para a Revisão da Tecnologia Jurídica no Século XXI, Elsevier 2009 Rio de Janeiro

Weiser M, Brown JS (1995) Designing calm technology. http://www.ubiq.com/hypertext/weiser/calmtech/calmtech.htm

Zittrain J (2008) The future of Internet and how to stop it. Yale University Press, Harrisonburg